Bloggerati, Twitterati

Bloggerati, Twitterati

How Blogs and Twitter Are Transforming Popular Culture

Mary Cross

 PRAEGER

AN IMPRINT OF ABC-CLIO, LLC
Santa Barbara, California • Denver, Colorado • Oxford, England

Library of Congress Cataloging-in-Publication Data

Cross, Mary, 1934–
    Bloggerati, twitterati : how blogs and Twitter are transforming popular culture / Mary Cross.
        p. cm.
    Includes bibliographical references and index.
    ISBN 978-0-313-38484-4 (hbk. : alk. paper) — ISBN 978-0-313-38485-1 (ebook)
1. Internet—Social aspects.   2. Blogs—Social aspects.   3. Twitter.   4. Popular culture.
    I. Title.
    HM851.C75   2011
    303.48'33—dc22   2011007447

ISBN: 978-0-313-38484-4
EISBN: 978-0-313-38485-1

15   14   13   12   2   3   4   5

This book is also available on the World Wide Web as an eBook.
Visit www.abc-clio.com for details.

Praeger
An Imprint of ABC-CLIO, LLC

ABC-CLIO, LLC
130 Cremona Drive, P.O. Box 1911
Santa Barbara, California 93116-1911

This book is printed on acid-free paper ∞

Manufactured in the United States of America

*For digital natives Stetson, Noah,
Max, and Annika*

Contents

Timeline of the Internet, Blogs, and Twitter

1957	In October, Russia launches Sputnik, the first spaceship to orbit the earth, leaving the United States behind in the technology race.
1958	United States organizes Advanced Research Projects Agency (ARPA) and subsidiary Information Processing Technology Office (IPTO) to move ahead on technology projects like interconnecting military computers at the Pentagon.
1968–1969	ARPANET network launched, using packet switching and hierarchical routing, which would be basics for the development of the Internet.
1971	E-mail developed by Ray Tomlinson, who set the protocol for using "@" in e-mail addresses.
1973	First trans-Atlantic connection on ARPANET, to University College of London.
1974	Beginning of Transmission Control Protocol (TCP) and Internet Protocol (IP).
	First use of term *Internet* for single global TCP/IP network.
1977	PC modem developed by Dennis Hayes and Dale Heatherington.
1979	Usenet launched, an Internet-based discussion system that allowed people to post public messages.
	Multi-User Dungeon (MUD) launches with text-based virtual worlds, role-playing games.

1983   ARPANET computers switch over to TCP and IP.

1984   Domain name system introduced (instead of numerical IP address).

1986   Protocol wars: conflict between European Open Systems Interconnection (OSI) versus U.S Internet/ARPANET protocol.

1988   Internet Relay Chat (IRC) allows real-time chat and instant messaging programs.

1989   America On Line (AOL) is launched.

World Wide Web written by Tim Berners-Lee, a global hypertext system using hypertext markup language (HTML), hypertext transfer protocol (HTTP), and universal resource identifiers (URLs).

1990   First dial-up Internet service provider (ISP), The World.

First Internet search engine, Archie (followed by Gopher in 1991).

1991   First web page, nxoc01.cern.ch, maintained by Tim Berners-Lee and Robert Cailliau.

First webcam, a video-capture device, monitored a coffee-maker at Cambridge University in England so workers could see if there was any coffee left.

MP3 file format launched to share songs and entire albums.

1993   Mosaic, first graphical web browser for public, devised by Marc Andreessen. Became Netscape, dominant web browser, which was then overtaken by Internet Explorer, shipped with Windows by 1997.

1995   Michael Sippey begins publishing "Stating the Obvious," weekly essays about the Internet and technology.

1996   First mobile phone, the Nokia 9000 Communicator, launched in Finland.

1997   Jorn Barger posts first weblog, calls new site *Robot Wisdom WebLog*.

1998   Google search engine launched, founded by Sergey Brin and Larry Page in Silicon Valley.

First news story broken online, not on mainstream media, by Matt Drudge at his *Drudge Report* about shenanigans in the White House during the Clinton administration.

2000	407 million users on Internet.
	Dot.com bubble, as investors and businesses rush to get in on the new Silicon Valley business model.
2001	Dot.com bubble bursts as value of sites sinks.
	Blogger William Quick claims to have invented the term *blog*.
	Research in Motion launches mobile phone email system for BlackBerry.
	Wikipedia, free online encyclopedia, launched by Jimmy Wales.
2003	MySpace begins, once the most popular social network.
2004	Facebook launched as college social network by Mark Zuckerberg.
2005	YouTube launched for free online video sharing.
2006	Twitter launches. First message, by Jack Dorsey, cofounder: "just setting up my twittr."
2007	Apple introduces the iPhone.
2008	First "Internet election," with presidential candidates Barack Obama and Hillary Clinton using the Internet to raise funds and gain supporters.
2009	40th anniversary of the Internet.
2010	1,966,514,816 people worldwide are on the Internet.
	Apple launches the iPad, sells more than 3 million in first four months, 15 million in one year, and launches iPad2 in March 2011.

ONE

Introduction

Blogs, Twitter, and Popular Culture

"Everything's changing!" a startled *Today* show news anchor blurted out, blinking into the camera as she finished reading the morning's headlines.

It's true. Nothing's going to be the same.

A tsunami of electronic media has overtaken us on the Internet, transforming everything in its path. It's a revolution, and no one quite knows where we are headed.

Way back in the 20th century, media guru Marshall McLuhan predicted that electronic technology was going to change the world, turning it into a village and sending people back to their tribes.[1]

Hello.

It's already happened.

In the 21st century of the blog, Twitter, and social media networks, we are already living in a global village online, sorting ourselves out into tribes of opinion, lifestyle, and ideology. If how people communicate determines how they think, live, and behave, as McLuhan said, we are well on our way to cataclysmic changes in those ways of thinking, living, and behaving. It feels as if the whole world is on the cusp of monumental change, at "an uncharted frontier," as *New York Times* columnist Frank Rich characterized it.[2] Maybe that *www* web address stands for the wild, wild web.

Blogs, Twitter, and social media networks on the World Wide Web have opened up the conversation and leveled the playing field for ordinary people to express themselves without the usual gatekeepers. Bloggers of every description and ideological stripe put out news bulletins and op-eds on a relentless hourly basis, covering everything from current events and politics to gossip, parenting, fly fishing, Jimmy Choo shoes, gambling, and much, much more. Twitter, the 140-character message hot spot, allows everyone from Joe the plumber to Lady Gaga to record their every thought and movement. Twitterati are first responders whenever there's a crisis, and Twitter has become the first place to look for an eyewitness account of whatever's happening. Celebrity Twitterati in Los Angeles tweet away about earthquakes, while New Yorkers worry about a mosque at Ground Zero and lament LeBron's decision to go elsewhere. Around the world, nearly 200 million people a month are posting updates on Twitter at an average rate of 140 million a day, 1 billion a week. Reports of the earthquake and tsunami in Japan and the uprisings in Egypt and Libya came out first on Twitter. Twitterati were first to report on crises like the "miracle on the Hudson" landing of a bird-stalled jet and the low-flying 747 Air Force One plane tailed by fighter jets over Lower Manhattan, which terrorized office workers with 9/11 déjà vu in 2009. Constant Twitter updates on current events, conferences, even breakfast menus are changing the rules of how we engage with the world and other people. It's wicked fast for one thing, it's interactive (TV is one-way), and for a no-attention-span audience, it's perfect.

Take the media event involving a Jet Blue flight attendant during a slow news week in August 2010. Steven Slater, now the most famous flight attendant in the world, was sporting a gash on his forehead from the errant suitcase of a passenger and mad as hell over her curses and rude behavior. As the plane landed, he reached the tipping point. Cursing out the whole plane of passengers over the public address system, Slater grabbed his bag and a couple of beers from the galley fridge, launched the evacuation slide, slid down it, bag and beers in hand, and drove home to Queens. For his "take this job and shove it" action, Slater became a folk hero on the web. Twenty thousand Facebook friends generated 150,000 posts, and a "Free Steven Slater" page collected 15,000 fans. Twitter was aflame, blogs chortled, both cable and network news had a ball. People wrote ballads about him and posted them online. On its blog, *Blue Tales,* Jet Blue responded, "It wouldn't be fair for us to point out absurdities in other corners of the industry without acknowledging when it's about us. . . . Perhaps you heard a little story about one of our flight attendants? While we can't discuss the details of what is an ongoing investigation, plenty of others have already formed opinions on the matter. Like, the entire Internet."[3]

This is what happens on the web whenever a news or gossip item catches fire. Information grows exponentially, taking over and colonizing social media. It illustrates the explosive impact of the Internet, the basic digital infrastructure that connects vast networks of computers globally and that was originally invented for military use. The Internet is home to the World Wide Web, the part of the Internet system that enables browsers, social media, and general access to information. This, as *Harper's* senior editor Bill Wasik commented, has become "the de facto heart of American culture...the public space in which our most influential conversations transpire, in which our new celebrities are discovered and touted, in which fans are won and careers made."[4] It's true; more and more, people are living their lives in this new public square. Indeed, some claim that because of the explosion of this digital technology, our culture is undergoing the biggest shift since the Industrial Revolution. Make that the printing press.

Moreover, mobile devices like smartphones and the iPad have taken over from the computer to make it easier than ever for everybody to be always "on." Apple reported in the summer of 2010 that it was making more money on the iPhone than the Mac,[5] underscoring Steve Jobs's earlier pronouncement that the computer is on its way out. Indeed, mobile devices are the web surfers of choice these days. First thing in the morning, maybe before they're even out of bed, people are checking their cell phones for messages. Kids are complaining they don't get enough attention at home anymore. At dinner parties, between courses, some of the guests may be surreptitiously glancing at their BlackBerries and iPhones, texting, checking e-mail, browsing the web. People are doing it during meetings at work too, as if wherever they are online is more important than where they are physically. Even drivers on the turnpikes and thruways, including those driving 18-wheelers, are—frighteningly—tweeting, texting, and checking e-mail as they drive. People are already going to jail for this in England.

GAME CHANGE

What's going on? Are we all just living our lives online, real only if posted? It's important to ask what cultural changes have come with this move to cyberspace and how it is affecting our own behavior.

This book has been written in an effort to figure that out, not only with the Internet but specifically with 159 million plus bloggers, the bloggerati who post online commentaries on just about any subject you can think of, and the nearly 200 million a day (and counting) tweeters on Twitter, the Twitterati who condense their messages into haiku-like 140-character counts. If we include the 500 million "friends" on Facebook—and we sort of have to since that's 22 percent of everybody on the Internet, enough to populate a small country—people worldwide are spending enormous, unprecedented amounts of time online every day, at home, at work, and on the road.

How is American—and global—culture changing because of this new frontier? And what does it say about us as a culture that we've taken to blogging and Twittering at such speed? What's the big attraction?

Let's start with the fact that it's free. And much of the lure is the connectivity and the instant gratification, the thrill of being connected with people on a high-speed back-and-forth wavelength that's as good as being face to face (or, sometimes, better). This can get to be addictive. In fact, one of the first rehab programs for Internet addicts—ReSTART—has just opened up in Redmond, Washington.

It's also the ease and spontaneity of self-expression that blogging, Twittering, and posting on social media sites like Facebook allow. You can say what you want when you want. But the biggest attraction is that you have an audience. You're not just talking to yourself. Somebody out there—lots of somebodies if you've been "friending" on Facebook or building your followers on Twitter and your blog—are listening and responding to what you have to say.

This is the crucial difference for blogs, Twitter, and social media networks, that you have a built-in audience for your self-expression. Instead of writing in a diary for your eyes only, on Twitter and your blog, you are not just expressing yourself, you're performing for an audience, often an audience of complete strangers. They're going to reply and comment on your performance, rate it, critique it, love it or hate it. Where else can you get that?!

The sheer pleasure of talking about yourself and attracting attention for it is hard to resist. Twenty-five billion tweets were posted in 2010 alone, according to a Twitter survey. Your 15 minutes of fame can be recycled over and over as you post your tweets or your latest blog communiqué, assured they will be seen by large numbers of people. They will be. The head count of Twitterati and bloggerati is expanding as we speak. With more than 1.9 billion people on the Internet everyday, some 200 million of whom are posting 140 million tweets daily, 97K per second, according to Twitter, and an estimated 156 million and counting bloggers out there, someone is bound to be reading and listening.[6] You rack up followers on Twitter as a sign of your fame and popularity just as you add up friends on Facebook and the hits on your blog as a mark of your place in the statusphere.

THE DAILY ME

Social media networks like Twitter seem to legitimize talking about yourself. As Massachusetts Institute of Technology computer guru Nicholas Negroponte puts it, "It's the Daily Me."[7] Is it any wonder that narcissists are disproportionately attracted to them, like proverbial moths to the flame?

Where else but on Twitter can you announce that you just brushed your teeth or ate a bagel for breakfast and have anybody notice or care (maybe, maybe not)? Where else can you endlessly set forth your views on health care or politics but in the blog you're writing that's managed to lure its own audience of acolytes?

The American capacity for self-absorption looks colossal online, where the Twitterati let it all hang out, making public some of their most intimate moments. The concept of privacy starts to seem almost quaint as you read through tweets about the most basic of people's daily routines—"I got up this morning at 6 A.M. and took a shower." "Coffee just kicked in." "The dog peed on the living room rug." What we tend to forget is that everything we say on Twitter or in a blog or on social media stays there, on Google Search and archived in the Library of Congress. It's hard to change what you've said about yourself online.

Nonetheless, "We're all into self-enchantment," says *Elle* advice columnist E. Jean Carroll, noting that Facebook is like a "press agent for the masses." "We're so in love with ourselves and we're selling, selling, selling. Everything gets turned into an Oprah moment."[8] Indeed, the potential for marketing yourself—and your business—on Twitter and on blogs is huge. It's already hip for businesses, libraries, nonprofits, and government agencies to say, "Follow us on Twitter" or on Facebook, where self-promotion of a commercial kind is rampant. Followers and fans may not realize that their every move (and click of the "Like" button) is being tracked. Stores are using web tracking to gauge customer interest, Hollywood checks Twitter to find out how the movie did over the weekend, and restaurants, Broadway shows, and just about all other venues are devouring the feedback from online postings. Everything is quantifiable online; digital technology makes it possible to measure and take the pulse of it all.

In fact, because of this technology and its ability to monitor what we're doing, privacy is a major issue of the new digital age, one that Facebook and other social media sites are wrestling with. The blurring of lines between public and private is one of the most significant side effects of social media, bringing out everyone's hidden exhibitionist and secret desires, all for public consumption. People do seem less inhibited online, possibly because they can be anonymous or use a nickname or an assumed identity, or maybe because nobody can see them; other people seem farther away in an Internet exchange. Online, because they can't actually see each other, people have to rely on words to parse the personality and emotion of others. But behind a mask of anonymity or an invented identity, people also allow themselves to get angrier and say things they would not in person, "flaming" any opposition with verbal aggression. Trolls, people who just want to stir up controversy, abound. Anonymity, engineered into the Internet from the beginning, provides a shield for all kinds of transgressive behavior. No need to remind ourselves that Al-Qaeda uses the Internet too, or that hate sites have grown 20 percent with social networking,[9] or that cyberbullying is on the rise. At least social media networks now outnumber the porn sites.[10]

A POWER SHIFT

Has all this self-expression just been bottled up or stifled until now, when it finally found an outlet? The Internet makes it temptingly easy, effortless even, to publish your thoughts, whether in a blog, through a tweet, or on a Facebook wall. What's going on online is a gigantic power shift away from established authorities like editors, publishers, and media elite into uncharted realms of individualized expression. People can present themselves and their ideas in their own way, perhaps even assuming a new identity in the process. This, needless to say, has its downside. There's plenty of baloney and trivia being promulgated in blogs and on Twitter. It's "the amateur spirit run wild," as author Kurt Andersen says in *Reset*.[11]

But the public conversation has also been hugely enhanced by this outpouring of self-expression and commentary. With traditional gatekeepers out of the picture, talented and creative people who might never have been given a voice in the culture now have access. They can promote their groundbreaking ideas and daydreams, even publish their own books. The underdogs of society, those who have been relegated to the margins, the groups with the least power, have a chance to speak their piece, as Twitter campaigns and protests around the globe have shown. The world of information has been opened up to everybody. Now the ordinary citizen is in charge, not the guy on top. "It's about the many wresting power from the few," *Time* magazine commented in "You," its Person of the Year issue in 2006, celebrating the online community for "seizing the reins of the global media," "framing the new digital democracy," and "beating the pros at their own game."[12]

Without the gatekeepers, what we're getting online is unvarnished opinion and the gossipy underside and inside story of people and events. These things have always been there, but editors and established publications seldom allowed them a public airing. Now, in this unrestricted public forum, the backstories are coming out, and the word of mouth can be heard. Information about what people are really thinking and what really happened is sometimes a whole different story than the official or published versions. The disconnect can be big. Celebrities and prominent people are learning to keep their mouths shut. In the now-24/7 news cycle, somebody is going to report what they said or did and post it on the Internet. People like General Stanley McChrystal, fired as commander in Afghanistan for comments a reporter published in *Rolling Stone,* are learning this the hard way. Bill Clinton, spouting off to a citizen journalist he didn't realize had a tape recorder, got to see his words go viral on the *Huffington Post.*

But the evolving online environment is also a very rich, complex, and satisfying place, so much so that one recent poll showed that 31 percent of single Americans online even said they thought the Internet could take the place of a significant other.[13] For some devotees, it does appear that life is largely being lived online. Online gaming is huge, 20 million people strong, 58 percent of whom are men, putting in something like 17 billion hours just on Xbox Live alone.[14] As Tom Funk observes in *Web 2.0 and Beyond,* the hours people spend on the Internet have "eaten into so many other leisure time activities," including relationships with flesh-and-blood people.[15]

Yet the new interconnectedness and access to information that blogs, Twitter, and the Internet make possible are also fostering a new sense of community and a new level of awareness. Even though most people say they go online for entertainment rather than for the news, we all have the opportunity to be better informed because of the information on the Internet. What's more, we can discuss it in whatever online forum we choose, whether a blog or a Twitter post or a comment at the end of someone else's blog.

A PARADIGM SHIFT

Thomas Kuhn, in his book *The Structure of Scientific Revolutions,* speaks of "paradigm shifts" that mark scientific discoveries, such as the shift from the Ptolemaic view of the earth as the center of the universe to the Copernican sun-centered model, or what would happen to our world-view if life were discovered on Mars. These radical shifts are the kind that readjust our concept of reality, a "conceptual transposition" where our understanding of the world is changed and replaced by another.[16] Although Kuhn was talking about science, his term *paradigm shift* has been applied to many other areas of human experience. It is an especially relevant term for the radical transformation taking place now with the Internet. In a paradigm shift, old ideas and institutions fall by the wayside as a new worldview takes over. Right now, just about every established element of our culture is under siege. Categories are shattering, institutions crumbling, destabilizing everything. Traditional newspapers and publishers are freaking out about their possible demise in the face of Internet-based news and e-books and are rapidly trying to regear for the new online age. Magazines are going under or revamping their pages for the iPad. Advertising, already suffering in a difficult economy, is scrambling to get back in the game on the Internet. The music business has already had its meltdown as consumers now download their own tunes and albums to their iPods and let CDs languish at the store. Restaurants complain about the instant, not-always-positive reviews customers can post online at Yelp.com after their meal. The U.S. Post Office, losing postal business to the Internet, is threatened and wants to cut mail delivery to just five days a week and raise the price of a stamp. Even credit card companies are being challenged by online pay sites like the one Google is setting up to bypass the plastic.

Mobile devices are making inroads on the computer itself. People prefer to check Twitter and social media on the go on their smartphones rather than be stuck at a computer on a desk. A Nielsen study showed that the time people spent on social networks, games, and blogs exceeded that spent on e-mail for the first time in 2009,[17] and the chief operating officer (COO) of Facebook, Sheryl Sandberg, has predicted the end of e-mail as social media sites take its place (e-mail, largely the province of an older demographic, is scorned by younger generations).[18] Futurists are busy predicting the arrival of artificial intelligence, and Google is hard at work to bring that about. Cloud computing, where servers take the place of the software and browsers we now use to get online, is launching. Someday you won't need anything but an iPad or a cell phone to do the work you now do on a computer.

A movement called the Singularity, partly underwritten by Google and heavily populated with Silicon Valley tech nerds, foresees a time when technology will take over from humans, replacing biology and the brain with enhanced versions that will extend life to up to 700 years. Raymond

Kurzweil, the movement's chief spokesman, claims that "within a few decades, machine intelligence will surpass human intelligence, leading to The Singularity—technological change so rapid and profound it represents a rupture in the fabric of human history. The implications include the merger of biological and nonbiological intelligence, immortal software-based humans, and ultra-high levels of intelligence that expand outward in the universe at the speed of light."[19]

Further, Kurzweil says, "The paradigm shift times are doubling every decade. ... So, the technological progress in the twenty-first century will be equivalent to what would require (in the linear view) on the order of 200 centuries. In contrast, the twentieth century saw only about 25 years of progress (again at today's rate of progress) since we have been speeding up in current rates. So the twenty-first century will see almost a thousand times greater technological change than its predecessor."

Science fiction? Not according to converts, who predict that the Singularity will arrive in 20 years. By 2030, they say, we'll be able to decode and manipulate DNA, regenerate our organs, and back up our brains.[20] Stay tuned.

ARE YOU ANALOG OR DIGITAL?

The whole world of information, accessed for 600 years on the printed page, is suddenly at our fingertips online, taking different forms and in its immediacy affecting how we use it. For one thing, information on the Internet isn't linear or sequential anymore; it's a spiderweb of links. It's digital, not analog. We track down data in an online dynamic of connections that can change by the minute. "Americans acclimated to clicking around hundreds of cable channels or Web pages experience the world less chronologically than their parents did," Matt Bai observed in a *New York Times Magazine* article about the president's multitasking agenda, "a complicated, eclectic agenda [that] suits our multitasking digital age."[21]

The naysayers are busy, just as they were when the telegraph and telephone, the railroad, the automobile, and television came on the scene. Some Internet critics are predicting that we're experiencing a general dumbing down because of the asynchronic activity that search engines like Google are training us for. A British baroness who is a professor at Cambridge warns that the younger generation is being reprogrammed by so much online activity (up to an average of eight hours a day for teenagers)[22] and American critics like Nicholas Carr say the Internet is training us to skim rather than read with sustained attention.[23] Jaron Lanier, author of *You Are*

Not a Gadget: A Manifesto, cautions that the programming design of the Internet itself, "locked in" long ago by engineers, may have unintended consequences.[24] Yet if you're an online habitué, have you ever taken a time out, a few hours or a day off from being online? It feels as if part of your brain is missing. But the constant interruptions and distractions of being on the Internet do take a toll, and, neuroscientists say, we need downtime to let our brains integrate our experience, the kind of thing that goes on when we sleep. Loren Frank, an assistant professor of physiology at the University of California-San Francisco, where a study of these Internet effects is in progress, says, "Almost certainly, downtime lets the brain go over experiences it's had, solidify them, and turn them into permanent long-term memories."[25] In other words, you, unplugged, are doing good things for your mood and memory.

We try in our own multitasking lives to juggle all kinds of out-of-order events and tasks simultaneously. We think we've learned to handle it, though several studies show that multitasking actually is less productive

"On the Internet, nobody knows you're a dog."

© Peter Steiner/The New Yorker Collection/www.cartoonbank.com

than we think.[26] Our lives on the Internet may deceptively foster the illusion that we've tamed the world. But with so much information coming at us, the distinctions we make between the real and the virtual, the truth and the fake, can get blurred and eroded, Lee Siegel says in *Against the Machine*. Information is becoming almost an ideology on the Internet, Siegel suggests, as knowledge *Wikipedia* style "withers away into information" and breaks down into "trival factoids."[27] In his book, *True Enough: Learning to Live in a Post-Fact Society,* Farhad Manjoo makes the point that "the deluge of information and our limitless choice of information have loosened our grip on what is or isn't true," which helps us "indulge our biases and preexisting beliefs," resulting in "a closeted view of the world."[28] We get to choose the information that suits us, in other words, and we may not be hearing other points of view.

Author and columnist for Truthdig.com Chris Hedges has the harshest words: "We've severed a connection with a reality-based culture, one in which we attempt to make fact the foundation for opinion and debate, and replaced it with a culture in which facts, opinions, lies and fantasy are interchangeable."[29]

It's Generational

Sysomos, a social media analytics company, surveyed 100 blog posts early in 2010 to uncover the demographics of bloggers in the United States and around the world. It found that the United States has the most bloggers, 29.2 percent, followed by Britain, with 6.7 percent, and Japan, with 4.8 percent. These bloggers are overwhelmingly young, with 21- to 35-year-olds doing 53.2 percent of blogging. Blogging is almost gender neutral: 50.9 percent of bloggers are women, and 49.1 percent are men.[30] A 2009 survey by Technorati, a blog search engine, found that 75 percent of U.S. bloggers are college educated, with one in three earning about $75,000 a year (this 2009 Technorati survey found that 60 percent of bloggers were men).[31]

According to another Sysomos survey, the majority of Twitterati are Americans, who contribute 50.88 percent of tweets, followed by Brazilians with 8.78 percent and British tweeters at 7.20 percent.[32] A study by Pew Internet Research showed that those who blog are also more likely to be on Twitter.[33] But, surprisingly, it's not the 16-year-olds among us who are tying up Twitter with their frantic tweets. Teens text, twenties Twitter. Teens are busy texting in their own cryptic language. It's the 20-somethings and above who Twitter, incessantly, obsessively even. When the whole system went down for a day and a half, hacked by some outlaws in eastern Europe, people didn't know what to do with themselves

The majority of those online on Twitter and Facebook are adults 25 to 34 and 45 to 54, who are twice as likely to use Twitter as a teenager, who is much more interested in connecting with friends than with the major issues in the news. But practically everybody under the age of 24 is, or has been, online. They are the digital natives, those born into the online world at the end of the 20th century. Twenty-five percent of Internet users are under 25.[34] Older users have been slower to adapt to new technology, but they are in the process of discovering it. At the moment, an eight-year-old third grader can run rings around his parents online.

THE DIGITAL DIVIDE

In all the excitement about Twitter, blogs, and social media, we tend to forget that many people are not online at all, ever. That's about 28 percent of the U.S. population right now. They either don't have access to a computer or, Luddite-like, refuse to have anything to do with one. In truth, the demographics of the writers of blogs and users of Twitter constitute a rather elitist group. The digital divide is also generational.

Digital natives, those born at the end of the 20th century into an online world, are all over the Internet. But the oldest members of the U.S. population have, within the last year, warmed to the digital world and are starting to go online with enthusiasm. A new Pew Internet and American Life report in August 2010 showed that social media use among people ages 50 and older doubled in the past year, from 22 to 44 percent.[35] In the European Union, 30 percent of the rural population has no access to high-speed Internet, and less than 50 percent of rurals in Greece, Poland, or Slovakia have it. The region with the lowest access is Africa, with 10.9 percent of the population online.[36]

Efforts by the White House and the Federal Communications Commission (FCC) to expand broadband coverage in the country and give schoolchildren and rural areas more access to the Internet are in progress. In the United States the demand for bandwidth doubles every two years, according to the FCC, which proposes to set up a system by the end of the next decade to run at 100 Mb a second (currently it is at three to four Mb). The FCC proposal, the National Broadband Plan, includes making available a new universal set-top box to connect to the Internet and cable service, and setting up a digital-literacy corps to train people to use the Internet. Needless to say, the broadcast and television industries are resisting the proposal, which would require auctioning off some of their spectrum to redirect to mobile Internet.[37]

The 2009 federal stimulus package, the American Recovery and Reinvestment Act, included $7.2 billion for broadband expansion projects. Some of this funding is beginning to trickle down to states. In addition, President Barack Obama signed a presidential memorandum in June 2010 aiming to double wireless communications in the next 10 years, making 500 megahertz of spectrum now in the hands of private companies and the federal government available for auction. While broadcasters returned 108 megahertz to the government when analog broadcast signals went digital, they are said to be wary of giving up any more, fearing it will just be warehoused.[38]

A Pew Hispanic Center survey in 2009 showed that mobile devices, cheaper than the cost of acquiring a laptop and installing broadband at home, have brought more Latinos and blacks onto the Internet, with 41 percent of Latinos and 51 percent of African Americans online. About a third of all Americans, the study showed, are going online on a cell phone "or other hand-held device."[39]

POLARIZING THE POPULACE

Notably, as we segregate into our tribal blogs and tweets online, the citizenry is becoming more polarized. Online, we naturally tend to read and respond to blogs that reflect our own views, "information that confirms our prejudices" and preexisting positions, as columnist Nicholas D. Kristof noted. This has the effect of insulating us in "our own hermetically sealed political chambers," Kristof commented.[40]

The Internet makes it easy to find your tribe and settle in with that ideology and political view. Surrounding yourself with people who think the way you do may feel cozy, but it can breed intolerance and extremism. The presidential election brought out some of the worst of that, and future elections will undoubtedly engender more of the same polarizing. Cable television and the networks have discovered that opinion-charged programming raises ratings; when viewers can detect political like-mindedness in a show, they tend to trust it more, rightly or wrongly. But this means people are closing themselves off from opposing or different views. Colin Powell said on *Face the Nation* in February 2010 that he thought the Internet and bloggers add to the tension between left and right. Tom Brokaw on the television program, *Morning Joe,* observed that the Internet offers everyone a constituency.

VIDEO KILLED THE RADIO STAR

Like graffiti on the sides of subway cars, the blogs and tweets proliferating on the Internet are making an indelible mark not only on pop culture but also on what's left of print journalism. It's a headline issue, debated daily in the pages of newspapers on the verge of bankruptcy. As blogs, tweets, and social media networks take over the Internet and a new generation gets all its news online, the question of what is going to happen to traditional journalism (even now known as "old media") is keeping journalists awake nights. Even the U.S. Senate has held hearings about the Internet's impact on news and newspapers.

Is the profession in meltdown? Has a counterculture of Twittering, blogging citizen journalists staked out so much territory on the web that established news sources can't compete? As digital media take over, one journalist predicted these may be the end times (pun intended) for print journalism. There is indeed a huge structural shift underway, propelled by technology and the changing behaviors it has given rise to, as an online populace of ordinary people revels in the interactivity and self-expression that the Internet makes possible, and the blog colonizes the territory of traditional journalism.

THE TINA *BEAST*

Former editor of *Vanity Fair* and the *New Yorker,* Tina Brown is now editor in chief of the *Daily Beast,* the online news and blog aggregator with its snazzy graphics and sexy "Buzz Board," "Big Fat Story," and "Cheat Sheet." She says she's finally "found a medium commensurate with my peculiar metabolism," one that lets her revel in "the immediacy, the responsiveness, the real-time-ness" of publishing daily on the web.

"It's a very exciting time in the culture," Brown says, "but a tough transition" as the world moves to digital daily life. "Things are moving at an incredible pace, but something new on Day One by Day Three is not so new." "It will shake out. Some will rise and flourish."

"We can now reach out to a public you couldn't reach before, all age groups," and she says she has been "creating new reporters—training and rigor are important, what you put into it." Brown says she looks for the "sharp, original, Beastly take" on politics, news, gossip, celebrities, and the arts.

At last count, the *Daily Beast* was pulling in 3.5 million readers monthly, and now has merged with *Newsweek* magazine with Tina Brown as editor-in-chief. Brown founded the *Daily Beast* in October 2008, using the name of a fictional newspaper from a novel by British author Evelyn Waugh, *Scoop*.

Author's personal interview with Tina Brown, December 9, 2009. *The Daily Beast:* http://www.thedailybeast.com

For example, leading up to an election in Iran, the worldwide Twitter messaging service was deluged with thousands of accounts of protests and street fights. Iranians, posting some 30 new messages a minute, turned Twitter into a virtual newscast for their cause, evading government restrictions and traditional state media. The government was forced into a game of whack-a-mole—as soon as it censored one Twitter feed, another popped up in its place. As the *New York Times* observed at the time, "The recognition that an Internet blogging service can affect history in an ancient Islamic country is a new-media milestone."[41] In Egypt and Libya in 2011, Twitter and bloggers became major conduits of information and organization during the protests.

Traditional publishers, watching Amazon's Kindle e-reader suck up their lists and profits, are frantically trying to retool the book business for this new age. The Google Books project to scan in every book in every library worldwide to one database strikes fear into the hearts of publishers, authors, and artists, who have already sued to protect their copyrights. Established bookstores, many already hit or going under in recent years as conglomerates take over, face their own possible extinction.

Things like this are happening faster than most of us can process, and we're not sure what it means or what it can lead to, this explosion of expression, this citizen journalism, this digital democracy. It has put print media and traditional journalists on suicide watch as whole populations suddenly find their own voice and seize the agenda. These voices have the potential to radically change global culture, not only by countering the dominant culture but also by creating an entirely new one.

THE NEW NORMAL

After the events of 9/11, we thought we had entered a "new normal" way of life. That is the question this book asks: What kind of culture will emerge from this radical transformation of established modes of communication?

As people learn new ways of experiencing and exchanging information, how will they and their way of life be changed? What will be considered the new normal?

Right now, it's hardly clear what normal will be or even if anything will ever feel like normal at the current Mach 2 rate of change. Technology has a life of its own, and what's happening is akin, perhaps, to the realization, once upon a time, that the world wasn't flat after all. The futurists are hard at work. Now that NASA has found water on the moon by torpedoing the dark side, the rush to forecast colonizing the moon has begun, and since climate change, bioterrorism, and nuclear war could make Earth uninhabitable, one space scientist suggests we might end up living in lava tubes with greenhouse-generated oxygen.[42]

We are in the middle of a revolution that is rapidly overthrowing our whole way of life. Let us investigate.

TWO

Popular Culture in a Digital Age

That fuzzy word *culture* has enjoyed unprecedented attention in recent years, but it has been a major heuristic for much longer. In our time, the word has been at the center of the so-called culture wars of ideology and politics both in the media and in the public, with the academic community chiming in frequently and loudly. Whole university departments of cultural studies ("cult stud" in the popular jargon) have sprung up.

Culture is indeed a contested and complicated concept. In some circles these days it has been generally taken to mean a lifestyle. According to Raymond Williams, the revered British culture guru who set about identifying the concept of culture and defining the word in the 1950s, culture is "a whole way of life," "incorporating meanings and values as they are lived and felt."[1] Simple and slightly vague, this has nonetheless turned out to be a working definition in academic circles and elsewhere. The word *culture* additionally has always had other meanings, Williams noted, as the "tending of natural growth" and as referring to "the general state of intellectual development" and "the general body of the arts."[2]

Further, as Williams observes, there has always been a distinction between high and low culture, with high culture designating the "intellectual or imaginative work" of "the inherited tradition,"[3] privileged as the highest and most worthy. The other was the common or popular culture from which emanate the everyday "tastes and lifestyles" of "the masses," "the many-headed multitude," as Williams put it.[4] Or, less elegantly, we might say pop culture is neon, and culture culture is a chandelier.

Ever since the Industrial Revolution and the development of mass media and a mass culture, however, there has been considerable blurring and slippage between these categories. The Museum of Modern Art (MoMA) shocked critics and the public in 1990 when it mounted an exhibition that displayed comic book art and advertising graphics next to revered works of modern art to show that transactions between high and low art and culture had been going on ever since cubism. Critics howled that the museum had abandoned its role as a discriminating cultural arbiter and called the exhibition a disaster.[5]

POP GOES THE CULTURE

That was 20 years ago. Now, used to seeing Jeff Koons's neon sculpture in Rockefeller Center and Lady Gaga everywhere you look, we wonder what all the fuss was about. MoMA has even added—"acquired"—for its collection the symbol @, the "at" sign, "*the* conjunction-junction of the computer age," as the *New York Times* put it.[6] Popular, so-called low culture has virtually taken over, and high culture has gotten itself locked up in museums and concert halls. If low culture was traditionally looked down upon (though MoMA cautiously redefined low culture at the time as "outside" culture), today it has become the dominant culture, not only in America but globally, bubbling up from below rather than coming from edicts on high, from the streets and ordinary people, and, now, especially now, from the information superhighway of the Internet. Artists take their cues from popular culture, fashion looks downtown for the next trend, advertisers track the brand preferences of the average grocery shopper, and politicians cannot afford to ignore the polls that tell them what ordinary citizens are thinking.

Traditionally, American culture has been thought of as a Western, Judeo-Christian culture, a whole way of life that values freedom, equality, individuality, and practicality. Though there have been multiple challenges to those values in recent years, the question that blogs, Twitter, and the Internet raise now is how will that culture change and what will define our social reality? What will be the values of a culture undergoing such cataclysmic changes?

American culture has already been transformed into global culture in many ways, and certainly the Internet itself has helped that happen. Yet American culture—the way we live, govern, communicate, and behave—remains distinctive. It is known the world over for its ideology of freedom and democracy, which, no matter how tarnished, seems to retain its utopian aura and exceptionalism. America, moreover, exports in its movies, music, television shows, and Internet sites the popular culture that has had a transformational, even threatening effect worldwide.

Popular culture at the magnitude of America is indeed a powerful force in the world, viewed as transgressive by many countries, as corrupting its youth and staining its heritage with trivia and distraction. British critic Dick Hebdige notes in his book about popular culture and postmodernism, *Hiding in the Light,* that British critics and educators regarded signs of "Americanization" and American cultural imports as "the beginning of the end" for British culture. For them, it was an "industrial barbarism" and "homogenizing" that would threaten Britain's whole way of life, coming as it did from "a country with no past and therefore no real culture, a country ruled by competition, profit and the drive to acquire."[7]

This reaction was typical of the hostility. Initially it was rock and roll that set the British off: "Come the day of judgment, there are a number of things for which the American music industry, followed (as always) panting and starry-eyed by our own, will find itself answerable for to St. Peter."[8] Fearing "the liquidation of the traditional value of the cultural heritage," as Walter Benjamin phrased it in *The Work of Art in the Age of Mechanical Reproduction,* the British perceived that what was at stake was their future.[9]

Popular culture is, in essence, the vernacular of America, where the populace holds sway and where entertainment and pleasure are important criteria, where "the great frame of life [may be] reduced to the flat dimensions of a comic strip frame, a television screen, a swinging ... social scene" and ignore categories of high art such as excellence, distinction, and uniqueness.[10] This is what Andy Warhol was picking up on in his pop art paintings of Brillo boxes and Campbell's soup cans. The term *pop art* itself didn't really gain currency until the early 1960s when postwar goods began to flood the markets, and the whole ethic of consumerism began to take hold.

It is *America's Got Talent* and *Jersey Shore,* Michael Jackson and MTV, tabloid newspapers and celebrity spottings, shopping malls and consumerism, conflicts about displaying the flag, prayer in schools, and the theory of evolution, issues of gender and gay marriage. It's Google searches and YouTube videos about Charlie Sheen's rants, the dangers of radiation plumes from Japan, the royal wedding, Lindsay Lohan in and out of jail, laughing babies, and sex tapes.

POP CULTURE, FROM BARNEY GOOGLE TO GOOGLE

Even though people may not have called it that, popular culture certainly existed long before the 20th century gave birth to the media and technology that made the concept something to reckon with. America was primarily a rural civilization in the mid-19th century, but after the Civil War, huge migrations of the populace and major industrial changes transformed the nation. It was becoming a nation of cities, as immigrants and natives alike moved from the fields into factory work, and technology and electricity began to change Americans' whole way of life. In the last decades of the 19th century and into the 20th, the invention of the telephone, the telegraph, the movies, and the phonograph; the mass production of the automobile; the transcontinental expansion of the railroad; the growth of corporations and mass merchandising; and a burgeoning press of daily newspapers created an entirely different kind of national culture, one that splintered and transformed older rural and small-town communities. It brought new affluence and allowed for "a new culture of leisure and materialism" as Robert Putnam tracks it in *Bowling Alone: The Collapse and Revival of American Community,*[11] with sports events and the invention of all kinds of cheap amusements, from nickelodeons to traveling carnivals, minstrel shows, vaudeville, dance halls, and dime novels.

The new mobility of the population, the new communications media, and the influx of foreign immigrants and emancipated blacks into cities meant huge social change, happening faster than ever before and breaking the old social bonds. People felt disconnected. Journalists and novelists like Jacob Riis, Lincoln Steffens, and Upton Sinclair decried the changes. But it created a new mix, a milieu of exciting contrasts and ambiguities that New York City denizens still prize.

By the time World War I began in 1914, American popular culture was a tangible if trivialized element of life. And, despite Prohibition, it thrived in the 1920s, with the invention of the technology of the radio and the first recognized radio station, KDKA in Pittsburgh, which broadcast election returns in November 1920. Owning a radio became a national obsession, homogenizing popular culture as television would do later.

Another unifying force was the daily comic strip, carried by most newspapers and featuring characters such as Krazy Kat, Mutt and Jeff, and a popular one named Barney Google. Sports like football and baseball, tennis and golf, swimming, and dancing became more accessible to ordinary people. Jazz music and dance crazes were popular entertainments.

Perhaps the biggest influence on popular culture was the movies, which came into their own in the 1920s with the introduction of sound and spread ideas about how people should look and behave. Walt Disney's Mickey Mouse became a popular icon in the 1930s. Magazines like *Life* and the *Saturday Evening Post* along with a thriving daily press offered coverage and interpretation of the news and fed the national fascination with stories about criminals like John Dillinger and Al Capone. During the Great Depression of the 1930s, radio was still king of the media. Orson Welles's 1938 radio drama, *The War of the Worlds,* which used simulated news broadcasts, panicked listeners, who thought there really was an invasion of aliens from Mars.

The 1940s brought America into World War II on two fronts, Europe and Japan. It was a time of rationing and patriotism, with staged air raid drills and civilian patrols, though the war never came to American soil. The movies were a primary source of entertainment and relief during the war years. When the war ended in 1945, returning GIs and their new brides settled suburbia and gave birth to the baby boom, with a record-breaking 76 million children born between the years 1946 and 1964, a cohort that was going to change the culture for the next half-century.

By 1953, two-thirds of American households owned a television set, a technology delayed by the war but one that rapidly took over leisure time, with shows like *Howdy Doody* and *I Love Lucy,* along with personalities like Milton Berle and Ed Sullivan. Though marked by the Cold War between the Soviet Union and the West (not a direct clash of armies but an ongoing dispute over postwar Europe) and the outbreak of the Korean War, the 1950s were a prosperous, relatively tranquil decade that saw the growth of the middle class, home ownership, suburbia, and college enrollment. A retired World War II general, Dwight Eisenhower, was president for two terms, and Elvis Presley gave rock and roll a prominent place on the music charts.

It was the calm before the storm of the 1960s, when coming-of-age baby boomers launched a counterculture revolt against middle-class morality and "the establishment." Protests at political conventions, takeovers of college campuses, and arrests ensued. The Vietnam War, telecast daily into everybody's living room, became a cause célèbre. Hippie-culture dropouts populated communes and participated in Woodstock, a four-day music festival. Major cultural changes were effected by the civil rights movement, the feminist movement and the entrance of women into the workplace, and the introduction of the birth control pill and the sexual revolution. The Beatles came to America, and the precursor of the Internet, ARPANET (Advanced Research Projects Agency Network), was launched in 1969, the same year as the first manned landing on the moon. Assassinations shocked the nation: that of President John F. Kennedy in 1963, and of Martin Luther King and the president's brother, Robert Kennedy, both in 1968.

Nothing slowed down in the 1970s except the economy, which limped along well into the beginning of the 1980s with rampant inflation and an oil crisis. Women were marching in the streets, burning their bras, and going to work under the banner of feminism. Divorce rates were climbing, social movements like environmentalism and gay rights took hold, and the music scene burgeoned with disco and soft rock. The first supercomputer was created, along with a prototype of the personal computer, the floppy disk, fiber optic cable, and the VCR. The World Trade Center twin towers went up in 1973.

By the 1980s, baby boomers had calmed down and become yuppies, taking jobs on Wall Street. IBM produced personal computers, the Berlin Wall came down, and the Cold War ended. Capitalism reigned, and a period of prosperity began, laced with drugs like cocaine. John Lennon was shot and killed. MTV and its music videos gave new prominence to musicians like Michael Jackson and Madonna.

Computer culture came into its own in the 1990s. At the beginning of the decade British engineer Tim Berners-Lee came up with an idea for a web of hypertext documents that became the World Wide Web. Apple introduced the iMac, Microsoft Windows populated just about every PC, and browsers like Netscape and Internet Explorer made web surfing easy. Hotmail made e-mail popular. The CD-ROM, DVD, and MP3 player came on the scene. As the decade came to a close, the transition to the year 2000 (known as Y2K) raised fears of a disastrous computer shutdown, but nothing happened. Meanwhile, Federal Reserve chairman Alan Greenspan warned of "irrational exuberance" as the stock market took off. Tiger Woods won his first big golf tournament, the Masters. In music, grunge and electronica took over. A Republican-run Congress tried to impeach President Bill Clinton for lying about an affair with an intern.

The millennium arrived, not with a bang but a whimper. The first decade of the 21st century was a great decade for techies, not counting the dot.com bust that started it off. Everything from Google and the iPod to Facebook, YouTube, Twitter, and the blog established themselves online, along with *Wikipedia,* Craigslist, and eBay. Smartphones and the iPad, WiFi and GPS all became omnipresent. The digital revolution was well underway, along with the switch from analog to digital television, the advent of the flat screen TV, and cloud computing. But the attack on the World Trade Center of September 11, 2001, seemed to change the world. Terrorists got on the Internet and planned more attacks, and the United States launched two wars in the Middle East to try to stop them. A Great Recession beginning in 2008 took down the stock market, several major brokerage houses, and the housing market itself. Unemployment lingered at 10 percent.

But, as Robert Putnam sums up in his study of community and social interaction in *Bowling Alone,* "No sector of American society will have more influence on the future state of our social capital than the electronic mass media and especially the Internet."[12]

THICK DESCRIPTION

To unearth clues about a culture, anthropologists seek out the "conceptual structures" and "established codes" of a society, as renowned anthropologist Clifford Geertz explains in his groundbreaking book, *The Interpretation of Cultures.* Geertz names the procedures of anthropologists in their "jungle field work" as "ethnography" or an "ethnographic algorithm." This is better defined, he says, as "thick description," the cataloguing of "inference and implication through which an ethnographer is continually trying to pick his way" in analyzing a culture.[13]

In this book, we are going to assemble a thick description, an informal ethnography, of the digital culture we're moving into via the Internet. As Geertz warns, however, "cultural analysis is guessing at meanings," not mapping the "Continent of Meaning."[14] Trying to interpret a culture while it is still in gestation is even more a matter of guesswork.

A revolution in culture is indeed unfolding, predicted by numerous media experts from Marshall McLuhan to the present day. New York University professor and media critic Neil Postman described the nature of this revolution in his book *Technopoly: The Surrender of Culture to Technology:* "A new technology does not add or subtract something. It changes everything," altering "the structure of our interests, the things we think *about,*" "the character of our symbols, the things we think *with,*" and "the nature of community: the arena in which thoughts develop."[15] Postman was writing in the 1990s about the computer itself, but he could well have been describing the evolving social milieu of our lives on the Internet, where the interconnectedness of people and information has indeed changed the nature of community, what we think about, and how our thoughts develop.

DESCRIBING DIGITAL CULTURE

We are already experiencing the cultural effects of the digital revolution that is underway. Here are some major effects, to be explored further:

- **Too Much Information**

  Because of new technology, information is coming at us in unprecedented amounts. The average American on an average day consumes 34 gigabytes and 100,000 words of information, according to an updated 2009 University of California-San Diego report, "How Much Information?" That's "the equivalent of about one-fifth of a notebook computer's hard drive depending on the model," the report said. The yearly total of U.S. information consumption added up to approximately 3.6 zettabytes (1 zettabyte is 1,000,000,000 trillion bytes).[16] The report included television, movies, radio, cell phones, video games, and reading the newspaper in addition to surfing the Internet.

Neil Postman predicted this. He said that the time would come when information would be regarded as a commodity, something to be bought and sold and turned into entertainment. "We are glutted with information, drowning in information, have no control over it, don't know what to do with it."[17] There is so much information that it tends to fragment our attention. Rumors are rife on the web, facts are sometimes slippery, and hate speech has found a forum.

On the plus side, however, we have access to information as never before about nearly everything in the world: current events, opinions, weather, history, our friends' and followers' messages, and reviews of restaurants, movies, theater, television shows, videos, games, music, and more. We can tell people where we are with a website, find directions with another, look for a date or a mate, find a place for dinner tonight, or book travel for next winter. Overall, we are better informed and better connected despite the deluge of information we live in.

- **The Revolution Has Gone Mobile**

The most radical cultural shift right now is that people are accessing so much of that information on a mobile device, not on a computer. Mobile devices *are* their computers. With the Internet in their pockets, accessing the web, Twitter, blogs, e-mail, and all those apps on a BlackBerry or smartphone on the go is a slam dunk. Steve Jobs of Apple has predicted that the personal computer is going to go the way of the farm truck, but CEO Steven Ballmer of Microsoft says no way: "The PC as we know it will continue to morph."[18]

A report from the International Telecommunications Union shows that 67 percent of the world's population (6.8 billion) now has cell phone access, and the United Nations predicts there will be five billion cell phone subscriptions worldwide in 2010.[19] The *New York Times* noted that "the fastest adoption of cell phone use is occurring in some of the world's poorest places," like Africa.[20]

Still, while everyone's using cell phones, not as many are talking, as another *New York Times* article announced, reporting a survey by the Cellular Telecommunications Industry Association (CTIA), which showed that although some 90 percent of U.S. households have a cell phone, less than half the traffic on them is phone calls. Instead, people are using cell phones to send text messages and e-mail, surf the Internet, listen to music, play games, and watch television.[21] Two-thirds of Hispanics and African Americans in the United States access the Internet via a mobile device, according to the Pew Internet and American Life Project in 2010.[22]

Broadband access is improving, as the Federal Communications Commission moves to add service to rural areas of the United States and speed it up everywhere. In 2010, more than 1.9 billion people worldwide had broadband access.[23]

- **The Culture of the Overshare**

The interactivity and the amount of sharing and disclosure going on via the web are stunning. Facebook has 500 million users and counting, there were an estimated 159 million blogs posted to the web by the spring of 2011 (with more than 68,000 new blogs posted every 24 hours),[24] and Twitter has more than 200 million users. What's astonishing is how fast the public has taken to these new media forms and in what numbers.

Even more astonishing is the amount of personal information people are revealing on these sites. Millions are spilling their guts online, telling the world what they had for breakfast or what the dog did or about a breakup with a boyfriend. The online anonymity built into the web makes it seem like another world, one where you can be whoever you want and say whatever you want. It's free, and there's no supervision. This is a major power shift, from established arbiters to ordinary people. The "hive mind" has taken over. In this new world, you can keep up with friends, find old ones, create a new identity, cultivate your image, and promote your book or your business, all without interference from a higher up.

- **Public versus Private**

The online anonymity built into the web does make it seem like another world. On Twitter, blogs, and social media and online in general, social norms tend to go by the wayside, and anonymity seems to cover over privacy concerns. But everything is public, and it stays there. The Library of Congress is already archiving tweets, and Google has added them to its search function.

Still, whether using their right names or an alias, people feel comfortable disclosing all kinds of personal information, unaware perhaps—or not caring—that it can be tracked, viewed, and archived. Social media are becoming increasingly commercialized, as the business world realizes the potential for branding and reaching consumers. With the "Like" button on Facebook, Twitter, and many blogs, the private lives, opinions, and preferences of people online are going public and becoming accessible to retailers, advertisers, and corporations. The privacy issues are, and continue to be, huge. Facebook is still sorting this out.

- **New Media**

In one sense, this digital revolution is all about media, the "intervening substance through which something is transmitted," as the *American Heritage* dictionary says, "the agency by which something is conveyed," the "means of mass communication." The media are front and center in this revolution as the Internet becomes "the agency by which something is conveyed." In fact, the media industry is growing faster than the U.S. economy itself, with its projected 6.1 percent average annual growth beating the 5.8 percent average rate for the U.S. gross domestic product, according to one media industry investment firm. "Spending on media and communications will outpace economic growth as consumers invest in mobile and Web access and companies pay to reach them there," private equity firm Veronis Suhler Stevenson (VSS) reported.[25] Old media like newspapers, magazines, and books are under siege in the digital revolution. It's a total game change for established media, and their survival is a matter of reinventing themselves for the online audience. Amazon made history in 2010 as it began to sell more e-books than hardcovers. Journalists, editors, publishers, authors, and even bookstores are threatened and are trying to retool, with paywalls, e-readers, and more. Barnes & Noble put itself up for sale, and Borders filed for bankruptcy.

Moreover, the rise of the citizen journalist on the scene, armed with a cell phone, makes hash out of a traditional newspaper's slower take on breaking news. Eyewitness accounts of crises and breaking news are faster and more compelling, if not always as complete or accurate. "Fast," however, is one of the problems. In a 24/7 news cycle moving at Mach 2, the need for speed and the sheer one-upmanship of the competition forces some information into the headlines without proper vetting, as, for example, in the media circus over a Department of Agriculture employee's otherwise-unremarkable speech in the summer of 2010, which ended up embarrassing the White House.

- **Politics and the Internet**

As the 2008 presidential election showed, using social media is a very effective way for a politician to get the message out and mobilize the electorate. Barack Obama ran rings around Hillary Clinton online, using Facebook and his own websites to recruit voters and funding. Such on-line communicating will be even more influential in future elections.

Yet politicians may have to be more guarded in what they say because of the intense online scrutiny and reporting they are subject to. Too many have been caught saying something they shouldn't have, taken out of context by the press, as they later claim.

In addition, the American public is becoming more polarized because of the Internet, where everyone can find a website, blog, or hashtag on Twitter that echoes their own views. Blogs and news outlets tend to play this up, realizing that their echo of public views can increase ratings and make them seem more accurate and trustworthy.

Moreover, in blogs and online news outlets and on television, media are becoming increasingly self-referential, reporting on and talking to each other. News often becomes what another media outlet did or said. And, startlingly, the media are increasingly partisan, taking sides in a way that the Fourth Estate of journalism traditionally abjured. But we're talking the Fifth Estate online these days.

- **The Long Tail**

In his much-cited book *The Long Tail, Wired* editor Chris Anderson pro-posed a theory about how business in a digital culture could profit from offering what he called a "long tail" of infinite choice, one that went way beyond the "head" of the beast of popular and trendy items to offer things only a few might want. Because the Internet is spawning a fragmented market of super-niched customers and cheap and easy distribution, busi-nesses can keep large inventories and profit from them by selling "less of more."[26] For example, Amazon, iTunes, and Netflix all offer long tails of products that continue to generate revenue even though only a few are buying at the far end of the tail. You can still find an obscure tome about Henry James's style, or a garage band's one album, or a restored Antonioni film from 1955 on these sites.

Anderson's book is a report on the progress of capitalism, but it under-scores in economics what is happening in culture, journalism, politics, and everyday life. "When mass culture breaks apart," Anderson writes, "it doesn't re-form into a different mass. Instead, it turns into millions of microcultures, which coexist and interact in a baffling array of ways." In effect, we are living in a *"massively parallel culture,"* one where we belong to many overlapping tribes at once.[27]

We will be investigating these issues and effects in more detail. Let us turn now to two of the principal promulgators of information, blogs and Twitter.

THE CULTURE OF THE BLOG AND THE TWEET

Once a product of the counterculture, blogging and Twittering have, in sheer size and influence, gone decidedly mainstream. Reading, writing, and discussing on Twitter and blogs are already a whole way of life for at least 77 percent of active Internet users and readers.[28] Countering the dominant culture of the institutional and the sanctioned rhetoric, blogs have created an entirely new one, opening up the public discourse to anyone from professional journalists to moms to the ordinary Joe to sound off on whatever, with topics ranging from political issues to diapering a baby. They offer the backstory, the inside story, the things everyone was actually thinking but had nowhere before to say. It's like "word of mouth on steroids," as Simon Clift, former marketing chief of Unilever, characterized it.[29] In this kind of radical power shift, blogs and Twitter also offer new channels of distribution for news, opinion, commerce, and, especially, entertainment. Just as most music now is available online (where buyers can simply buy or purloin a song, leaving the once-strong music industry to cope as it may), movies, DVDs, games, sports events, television shows, and much more in our multiple-choice pop culture will increasingly move to the web where, complete with reviews and commentary by bloggers, these entertainments will be widely accessible (and coming to a TV near you).

To speak of culture in the blogosphere or the Twittersphere, words themselves needing definition as they are too new to make the last edition of Webster's, we need to talk about how these phenomena of blogging and tweeting are affecting how people live and conduct their daily lives. *Blogosphere* is a coinage (claimed by Biz Stone to have been thought up in 2002 by blogger William Quick)[30] that refers to the community of blogs, bloggers, and their readers, a world centered on the Internet (some have suggested the alternative term *Blogistan*). In the latest terminology according to Technorati, it's called an "ecosystem," one of "interconnected communities of bloggers and readers at the convergence of journalism and conversation."[31] In the United States alone, that ecosystem includes something like 31 percent of Internet users reading blogs, and 12 percent writing them, according to a Pew Internet report.[32] It's a little hard to define since it is estimated that more than 55,000 new blogs are created every day. Globally, the numbers are also difficult to come by as nobody's tracking them in a systematic way. For now, though, America is the capital of the blogosphere, with 29 percent of all blogs emanating from the United States.[33] Twitter, a much newer online phenomenon based on 140-character postings, has enjoyed phenomenal growth since it was launched in March 2006 by a trio of Internet geeks in California: Jack Dorsey, Biz Stone, and Evan Williams. Twitter initially was the province of techies. But it came of age in late November 2008 when hundreds of Twitter reports started coming in from the siege of two hotels in Mumbai, India, beating out traditional news organizations with frequent updates on the situation. Since then, although it is difficult to maintain an accurate count, an estimated three million messages are posted on Twitter every day on average, with an estimated one million plus users. Like haiku, which relies on a certain number of syllables, a posting on Twitter must remain within the 140-character count, a limit imposed to fit the text protocols of the short messaging system (SMS) on mobile devices. Followers can read and respond or join a hashtag #@ group of the like-minded. Part of the effort on Twitter is to build followers. By April 2011, Lady Gaga had 9.1 million followers on Twitter, beating out everybody including Britney Spears, President Obama, and Ashton Kutcher.[34]

It's hard to imagine what world culture will look like in a few years. As Aaron Barlow comments in his book *Blogging America: The New Public Sphere,* we are still "within the early days of the changes wrought by the Internet," and blogs are "a new cultural paradigm which we don't know yet what to call." Yet blogs as "a new and original cultural phenomenon" probably reflect more "the changes and needs in society" than the "simple realization of technological possibility."[35] In other words, we asked for it. Why have people taken to blogs and Twitter in such numbers and at such speed? What needs do they fulfill in our culture? The voice of the people is being heard more directly than ever, and the ordinary person's allotted 15 minutes of fame can be instantly bestowed by the blog, Twitter, and social networks like Facebook. The rise of reality shows on television and of call-in talk radio is not unrelated to this phenomena. And, certainly, the Internet has already laid down its own cultural foundations, in a global fashion. The connections between people and between countries have been increased by megawatts on the Internet, though it may, some warn, be decreasing the actual number of face-to-face encounters.

Essentially, a blog is like written conversation, creating an informal atmosphere that gives information the kind of immediacy and interaction that is more like a face-to-face encounter than a straight news story. Blogging is "writing out loud," as blogger Andrew Sullivan of the *Daily Beast/ Newsweek* characterized it, "more free-form, more accident-prone, less formal, more alive" than ordinary writing.[36] And, a crucial difference, it's public. The minute you put it out there on the web, it can hang around out there for a very long time, as some bloggers, tweeters, and Facebook-using job seekers have discovered to their dismay.

"THE NEWS HAS BECOME SOCIAL"

Arianna Huffington, co-founder and editor-in-chief of the *Huffington Post,* is running the fastest-growing news site on the web, with more than 24 million unique monthly visitors and a 94 percent year-over-year increase in unique visitor growth as it celebrates its fifth anniversary. Beginning as a blog aggregator, the *HuffPost* is morphing into a major Internet newspaper, adding established journalists to its 195 full-time staffers, celebrity columnists, and 6,000 volunteer bloggers. Social media sites include *HuffPost Social News* on Facebook and the *HuffPost Twitter Live Edition.* And now that it has been purchased by AOL, the *Huffington Post* will have an even greater reach.

Named one of the Most Powerful Women in the World by *Forbes* magazine in 2010, Huffington says that as new technology transforms our culture, it has enabled "millions of consumers to shift their focus from passive observation to active participation—from couch potato to self-expression." "Instead of watching TV for 8 hours straight," she notes, "people are weighing in on the issues—great and small—that interest them. Social media are helping people share, create, and connect ... rising above the narrow confines of our own individual concerns to the broader concerns of all humanity."

What's ahead for journalism in the new digital age? "Despite all the upheaval," Huffington says, "I believe the future of journalism is very bright. Indeed, we are living in a Golden Age for news consumers who can surf the net, use search engines, access the best stories from around the world, and be able to comment, interact, and form communities.

The Web has given us control over the news we consume. We are part of the evolution of a story now."

"In short," Huffington says, "the news has become social," She predicts it will become "even more community-powered ... collaboratively produced by editors and the community" with "conversations, opinion, and reader reactions seamlessly integrated into the news experience."

Author's Q. and A. with Arianna Huffington, October 12, 2010. *Arianna on Twitter:* @ariannahuff

The blog has, in effect, returned public conversation to the people and reestablished the public square, opening up the world of information to everyone. And, crucially, the blog has given writers an audience, one that talks back. The audience for blogs, as estimated in 2008 in an annual report by Technorati, is over 346 million readers worldwide.[37] We're talking blogosphere, a whole new world of communication and connection.

THE TWITTERSPHERE

If the blogosphere is the new public square, the Twittersphere is the new water cooler, generating instant connectivity, feedback, and a sense of the social. People have taken to it in droves, posting everything from diary entries, to nasty comments on other people, to recipes for elaborate foods, to comments and promotions for brands, movies, and Broadway shows. Twitter, which is really a microblog, has spawned dozens of add-ons and apps, a sign of its burgeoning popularity. Constant predictions of its imminent demise have proven greatly exaggerated.

Here in the age of the overshare, Twitter seems to play best to the narcissistic and attention junkies among us, fostering egocentric exchanges of trivia and inanity, but it also conveys vital information, updated news, and emergency bulletins. Twitterers can find a group of the like-minded simply by sending a tweet that attracts its own group of followers.

According to a *Harvard Business Review* study, only about 45 percent of Twitter users actually tweet, with half of the registered Twitterati tweeting less than once a day and 25 percent who don't tweet at all. About 10 percent of active users are responsible for over 90 percent of the tweets. Twitterati are mostly female—55 percent—and more than half tend to follow men. Sixty-five percent of the men on Twitter follow men, not women, according to the survey.[38] A survey by the website Mediabistro.com found that 10 percent of the women online are using Twitter, but only 7 percent of men online are.[39]

Inventing the Digital Self

These new ways of experiencing information and the new rules of engaging with it are changing people's behavior and their everyday lives. Just as the advent of television or the cell phone (or even the printing press) changed the way people lived, behaved, and connected with each other, these new digital technologies are making inroads on the collective psyche. Blogs and Twitter create instant audiences and feedback. Blogs have become daily must-reads for vast numbers of the online public, to say nothing of the journalists, politicians, pundits, and corporate marketers who cannot afford to miss what is being said outside of the established media.

With no editorial supervision, the blog and Twitter, while prone to the trivial and inane, nonetheless are major vehicles for new voices, new ideas, and new creativity. One thing is certain: The rate of change has reached an unprecedented speed, and it's affecting the way people think and behave.

By themselves, the Internet and the computer have already created a new culture. "The computer is a new mirror, the first psychological machine," Sherry Turkle of the Massachusetts Institute of Technology says in *Life on the Screen: Identity in the Age of the Internet,* offering us a compromise between our fears of being alone and disconnected and our fears of intimacy. On the computer, "You can be a loner, but never alone. You can interact, but need never feel vulnerable to another person." "Emblematic of the encounter between the machine and our emotional lives," computers "provoke us to think about who we are."[40]

One of the most compelling determinants of people's behavior on the Internet is the lure of anonymity, which seems to liberate people from the usual social norms and to offer new forms of identity. People can lead totally separate secret lives on the Internet, and they do, in "high tech solitude."[41]

The Tribes of the Internet

As Marshall McLuhan predicted would happen with the rise of electronic technology, people are gravitating online to the tribes of opinion, ideology, and lifestyle choices they identify with. The technology of the Internet and the computer is changing the way we choose our social groups, says Farhad Manjoo in *True Enough: Learning to Live in a Post-Fact Society.* We used to connect with others mostly by pure propinquity, he says. Now, our exposure through the Internet helps us choose the groups and the information that suit us. "We select our reality according to our biases."[42] The Obama administration, in trying to demonize Fox News as dangerously right-wing, faces a highly polarized, politicized electorate. But news organizations and websites have a vested interest in echoing their readers' and viewers' biases, since that tends to foster a sense in the audience that the source is accurate.[43] As the audience is fragmented according to such choices, Manjoo points out that public discussion becomes increasingly polarized, "facilitating a closeted view of the world, keeping us coiled tightly with those who share our ideas."[44] In other words, the way we sort ourselves out into social groups is being changed by technology. "People are re-forming into thousands of cultural tribes of interest," *Wired* editor Chris Anderson, author of *The Long Tail,* says. They are "connected less by geographic proximity and workplace chatter than by shared interests."[45] Or, as Bill Wasik notes in his book about the Internet, *And Then There's This,* these tribes are subcultures where they "converse incessantly among themselves in an intense, always on, inwardly directed banter," a crowd "talking and thinking about itself as if it were the center of the entire universe."[46]

The Internet is already becoming a primary source of news for many Americans, encouraging a closeted point of view because it lets people more easily filter out what they don't want to see or hear. Moreover, it's interactive; they can respond, comment, and share online news. According to a Pew Internet Research poll, 61 percent of Americans, or 6 out of 10, say they get at least some of their news from the Internet these days, as opposed to the 1990s when the majority watched nightly television news programs. Three-quarters of Americans say they hear of news via e-mail or updates on social media sites.[47]

Political patterns are clearly changing. No one has tabulated the number of left-wing and right-wing news sites on the web, but there are many to choose from. On the left, sites like the *Daily Kos, MoveOn.org, Media Matters, The Nation, Firedoglake, NPR,* the *Huffington Post, Time,* and *Newsweek* espouse a more liberal point of view. On the right, Fox News, the *Drudge Report,* the *Wall Street Journal,* the *Weekly Standard,* and the *New York Post* lean right, to say nothing of Rush Limbaugh, Ann Coulter, and Glenn Beck media sites. Though Americans traditionally have taken a centered, moderate approach, now on every political issue, Americans can find their niche and their tribe.

BORN DIGITAL

Let us turn now to the natives in this culture, in this case the digital natives. They are the kids born at the end of the 20th century who are growing up digital. None of them has yet grown into adulthood or lived to a ripe old age. No cradle-to-grave natives here to study in an ethnography. But they think the world has always been this way, wireless and at their fingertips on computers, netbooks, cell phones, and Kindles. They have known no other.

They can play video games like experts, and they text their friends at a rate of up to 100 messages a day. Your teenager isn't hogging your land-line, she's upstairs texting you about when dinner will be ready or asking for help with her homework. She doesn't bother with e-mail (so over) or Twitter. She doesn't spend a whole lot of time reading books at the library, but she can search Google and *Wikipedia* in a flash to do a term paper. If you need help with your computer, you ask her, but at least you did man-age early on to learn parental controls to block websites on hers and rein in her Facebook page.

The Internet isn't a very safe place for her right now. Kids her age haven't been worrying about privacy as their parents do, and the web is full of predatory types. While commercial entities on the web have a vested inter-est in keeping it safe for their own customers, there are plenty of ways they can't. Social media sites earn money by letting retailers and corporations have access to the personal information people divulge; bullies are all over the place, targeting their victims; and sweet-talking sickos, masquerading as teens, have lured more than one child to an unhappy ending.

By the time your digital daughter gets to college, her textbooks may all be e-books (hey, they'll be cheaper), customized for the class by her pro-fessor, embedded with the course syllabus and commentary, videos, and maybe even some new chapters. She can also sit in her dorm room in her pajamas and take some of her courses online, doing research in *Wikipedia,* the collaboratively written online encyclopedia in 270 languages with 16 million entries. She could get overwhelmed with the sheer amounts of information coming her way, her brain could wind up being differently wired, and she could become addicted to a digital life, perhaps missing out on real personal relationships.

As John Palfrey and Urs Gasser note in their study of this generation in *Born Digital,* digital natives are used to operating online without an authority stepping in. Nobody's in charge, the gatekeepers are absent, and they can do and say whatever they want. This kind of power shift, says Palfrey, tends to favor "the individual and the nimble, small ad hoc group as against the large, slow-moving institution," relating to "the long move-ment in history against certain forms of hierarchies."[48] The fact that "a greater number of people are able to tell the stories of their times" in the participatory environment of the Internet may mean that a "broader group of people participate in the 'recoding' and 'reworking' of cultural meaning." They will, Palfrey and Gasser predict, have "a profound and lasting impact on democracies." At the same time, this participatory digital culture can spawn angry partisanship, diminish the quality of discourse, and become increasingly colonized by commercial interests.[49] Even President Obama warned a graduating class in 2010 about the distractions of the "24/7 media environment" they were going to live and work in and the information they'll encounter that won't "rank all that high on the truth meter."[50]

By the time these digital natives are 20, Gasser notes, "They will have accumulated at least 10,000 hours as active users of the Internet," time "roughly equivalent to what a musician is expected to practice in order to become, say, a professional piano player or cellist."[51] Then there are the digital immigrants, the rest of us who are rapidly learning, of necessity or by desire, to live in the digital culture we suddenly find ourselves in. Astonishingly, the biggest surge in new Facebook users now is among 50- to 64-year-olds, who are crowding the site, connecting with long-lost friends and family members, and looking for new ones. We know that bloggers are mainly men in their thirties, and that those on Twitter are also younger men (but there are more women than men on Twitter).

Although Americans are now spending as much time using the Internet as watching television, they still spend 41 percent of their time watching television, itself transformed by digital culture. They still wear analog wristwatches and use analog landlines (though college students reportedly don't wear a wristwatch anymore because they tell time on their cell phones). The Luddites, once the term for a group of 19th-century British workers who destroyed new textile machinery for fear it would cost them their jobs, are still among us, people who shun the whole online world and refuse to use it. They are used to spending more contemplative time with a newspaper or a book. They still send handwritten thank-you notes, and they are not out buying Kindles. And there is still a big digital divide in America, where some 24 percent have no access to broadband or computers. This digital divide is also generational.

But there's a certain amount of inevitability to the encroachment of digital culture. As an old joke goes, one caterpillar says to another, watching a butterfly flit overhead, "You'll never get me up in one of those things."

THREE

Got Blog?

Blogs, those individual, idiosyncratic commentaries, usually written by one person or group (or, these days, corporations) and posted on a regular basis on the Internet, are a major phenomenon of digital culture. Starting out as voices of the counterculture, blogs have now gone mainstream. Indeed, blogs are "more mainstream than the so-called mainstream media ever was," Lee Siegel says in his assessment of culture and the Internet, *Against the Machine*.[1] On the Internet, the blogosphere has a wider reach and a larger audience than any media have ever had.

"Bloggers," as public relations guru Mark Penn comments, "are becoming the Fifth Estate" in America, giving the Fourth, the press, a run for its money.[2] Moreover, bloggers in the United States do 29.2 percent of all blogging worldwide, four times as much as in Britain, which ranks second with 6.75 percent.[3] BlogPulse, a Nielsen company that tracks blogs, found that worldwide, there were 158,273,691 "identified" blogs in existence on March 22, 2011, with 72,870 new blogs that day and more than 1.1 million blog posts in 24 hours.[4] The numbers go up faster than anybody can keep track. The 1999 weblog of blog originator Jorn Barger has come a long way in little more than a decade.

What's the attraction? Bloggers say that personal expression is far and away the reason they've started a blog, the chance to describe their personal experiences and have an audience for it. And blog readers themselves say the connection with that same personal experience and the chance to comment and hold a conversation about it are what keeps them coming back. Blogs, essentially, are "word of mouth on steroids," as one CEO put it,[5] a wisdom-of-the-crowd way to find out what's going on because they bypass officialdom and establishment gatekeepers and have more credibility as unfiltered news and opinion. Powerful influencers, bloggers are often the first to know the latest information. And they know how to jack up readership, embedding links and using controversy to hike up the hits.

For example, one of the most popular categories of blogs is the "mommy blog," dishing out advice and empathy on raising children. Mommy blogs are so popular they are becoming "a cultural force to be reckoned with," according to the *New York Times*.[6] Written by an ever-increasing number of the 82 million women in America with children under 18, these mommy blogs (and there are daddy blogs, too) describe in sometimes gory detail the ups and downs of parenting. Blogs like *Absolutely Bananas, Mom 101,* and *June Cleaver Nirvana* give the real-life story of raising kids, generating plenty of feedback (and, not incidentally, corporate interest). One mommy blogger in Philadelphia, a 33-year -old mother of two children, attracted 60,000 unique visitors a month to her website, Classymommy. com, in the summer of 2010.[7]

According to BlogPulse, some of the most popular blog topics in 2010 were movies and television, followed by sports, politics, and what are called "memes," those jokes, novelties ("LOL Cats"), and surveys ("Are You Spiderman?") gone viral that build links and rank in a blog.[8] Technorati, the blogosphere search site, shows politics as the top blog topic, followed by technology (second), celebrity/gossip (third), and business (fourth).[9] Pew Internet Research found that politics and foreign events are the top topics in the blogosphere. Science is third, followed by technology (#4), health and medicine (#5), and celebrity (#6).[10] A major item on blogs in 2010 was what was known as "climate-gate," the discovery of e-mails among scientists about possible manipulation of global climate research in Britain, a story that was then picked up by traditional media.

Bloggers skew young. Even kids are blogging. A 2010 Sysomos survey found that 53.3 percent of U.S. bloggers are 21- to 35-year-olds. Under-21 bloggers contribute 20.2 percent of blogs, and bloggers from 36 to 50 years old add 19.4 percent. But only 7.1 percent of those over 51 do any blogging. According to the same survey, bloggers in the United States are about evenly divided between men (49.0 percent) and women (50.9 percent).[11] However, a Pew Internet and American Life study found that blogging is declining among those under 30 as wireless connectivity rises in this age group. Social media like Facebook have taken over. "Blogging appears to have lost its luster for many young users," the author of the study, Amanda Lenhart, says.[12]

Today, an estimated 20 million bloggers of every description and ideological stripe put out news bulletins and op-eds on a relentless daily basis in America. California has the highest percentage of bloggers, 14.1 percent of the total, with New York state second at 7.1 percent, followed by Florida, Texas, and Washington State at 5 percent, and Massachusetts and Virginia at 4 percent.[13]

Blogging worldwide, as the June 2010 Sysomos survey showed, hasn't yet caught up to the United States and Britain, with Japan coming in third with 4.9 percent of all bloggers, followed by Brazil at 4.2 percent and Canada at 3.9 percent. In Europe, Germany leads with 3.3 percent blogging, followed by Italy (3.2%), Spain (3.1%), and France (2.9%). There were bloggers at a rate of 2.3 percent in Russia. Oddly, Indonesia and Australia have no bloggers, though their numbers of Internet users are high.[14] They like Twitter better. With the rise of mobile phones, especially in Asia, Twitter is the site of choice rather than blogs.[15]

WHAT DO BLOGGERS DO?

As Mark Penn notes, no tests or degrees are required to become a blogger, and so far, there's no regulation either.[16] If you want to start your own blog, all you have to do is go to a website like blogspot.com, blogger.com, or tumblr.com and open an account. It's free. Basically you will be setting up a simple website, featuring your own blog postings, arranged in reverse chronological order from most recent to earliest. Blogs are public (though you can restrict access somewhat), inviting others to become your audience and post their comments. To keep a blog going and keep it interesting, you have to update it often. And to give your blog Google prestige, it helps to display lots of links on it. Some bloggers go overtime cultivating those links ("Google bombing") and thereby upgrading their blogs' Google status, which is determined by popularity, not quality.

Blogs are collected online within RSS (really simple syndication) newsreader groupings like Blogger. Take a look at what the Blogistan or blogosphere, the community of linked blogs, looks like on the newsreader Bloglines, where you can get a overview of the "200 most popular feeds." These include some standard favorites like *Slate* magazine, *Salon,* the *New York Times Book Review* blogs, *The Daily Kos, Boing Boing, TMZ,* and, just for fun, *I Can Has Cheezburger?* about cats, *I Will Teach You to Be Rich,* the *Dilbert Daily Strip,* and Perez Hilton's celebrity gossip site. The most popular blog in 2010, according to Technorati, the blog search engine, was the *Huffington Post,* the news and blog aggregator founded by Arianna Huffington. Some blogs, like *Gawker,* the gossip site of blogs that defined the blogosphere for so long, are now turning themselves into full-fledged news sites, undergoing a redesign to use feature stories and bigger images in order to suit iPad viewing.[17] The *Huffington Post,* built on blogs and doubling its traffic in two years, has announced it wants to become "America's online newspaper."[18] Blogs cover everything from current events and politics to gossip, parenting, fly fishing, preteen fashion, and much, much more. The most prevalent kind of blogs are the personal ones, like diaries, "describing their personal experiences to a relatively small audience of readers," according to a Pew Internet and American Life Project research study.[19] Another study also found that 20 percent of American Internet users were using "digital tools"—blogs, e-mail, and social media—to talk to their neighbors and be part of a community.[20]

A "QUINTESSENTIAL BLOG"

Ronni Bennett, a computer consultant and a former producer for the *Barbara Walters Show* in New York City, now lives in Oregon and writes a highly successful, attention-getting blog, *Time Goes By,* all about the issues of getting older in America.

In six years of writing the blog, she has amassed a huge following that keeps her blog site at the top of the list for baby boomers and older (and younger) readers. Ronni coined the term *elderbloggers,* which is now, like *mommybloggers,* the label the mainstream media have adopted. The *Washington Post* called *Time Goes By* the "quintessential" elderblog, and the American Association of Retired Persons named Ronni the "dean" of elderbloggers for setting the standard.

Ronni says blogging is a seven-day-a-week job to constantly publish fresh material and keep up with the deluge of e-mail and commentary she receives on *Time Goes By.* Twelve-hour days are common. She is regularly consulted by government agencies about elder issues and invited to write articles and speak at conferences and on television and radio.

"Elders are the fastest-growing cohort going online," Ronni says, and "blogging has the potential to improve elderhood in many ways and many times over." It is "an almost perfect pastime," keeping minds active, widening interests, making friends. "In our later years," she says, "we want to put some serious thought to our lives, to the issues of the day. That can't be done in 140 characters."

At a time when the population of older Americans is expected to increase by 40 percent in the next five years, *Time Goes By* is well positioned to help them age gracefully.

Author's personal interview with Ronni Bennett, September 24, 2009. Blog address: http://www.timegoesby.net

But beyond the daily diaries and personal narratives, there are music blogs and wine blogs, Jimmy Choo shoe blogs, gambling blogs and pet blogs, blogs for seniors and blogs for those with newborns, Iraqi blogs, and stock market blogs. The archbishop of New York has his own blog, *God Is Everywhere, Even on the Blog.* Even the pope is online (with a page on Facebook). Colleges like Massachusetts Institute of Technology, Amherst, Yale, and Wellesley have started posting their students' blogs on the school website as a marketing move to give prospective applicants a taste of student life on campus. Goodwill, a charity organization to help the down-and-out, has bloggers in many parts of the country tout the bargains at their local thrift stores. The jury is still out on whether the army will allow its personnel to use social-networking sites and blogs, but there are underground bloggers even there. The Pentagon itself blogs, at *Small Wars Journal,* and Timothy Geithner, secretary of the Treasury, has invited bloggers in the financial industry to write and post blogs (a Treasury spokesman said blogs are particularly influential because reporters at traditional media tend to read them).[21] Hardhat bloggers, protesting the building of a mosque near Ground Zero in New York City in the summer of 2010, posted a "911 Hard Hat Pledge" on their *Blue Collar Corner* site of blogs, listing all the construction workers who said they would refuse to work on the building.[22] "I would die first before laying a brick on that job," said one.

Bloggers all over the world are making themselves known—and unwanted, as in China where they are frequently excised from the web. On a visit to China in 2009, President Obama invited a group of the most prominent Chinese bloggers to hear his speech at the Great Hall of the People in Beijing, but the Chinese government preempted him, disinviting the bloggers. Foreign governments, used to heavily monitoring information, are alarmed at losing control over what goes out unregulated on the web. The United Arab Emirates announced a ban on BlackBerries in 2010 because of "security concerns" (read: they can't monitor its encrypted data to screen for politically or morally objectionable material).[23] A week later, India too said it would shut down BlackBerry service if it was not granted access to encrypted data.[24]

In the Middle East, blogging is less regulated but dangerous. Reportedly, Iranian authorities have considered the death penalty for dissenting bloggers. Blogs (and Twitter), however, were faster than news agencies in getting the news out about the Iranian election protests in 2009. The Iranian government tried to stop them, shutting down the Internet, lowering bandwidth, and removing stories from the front pages of newspapers, which were published with large areas of white space where stories had been censored.

The Amish, a sect of Christian Mennonites who spurn electricity and zippers, are perhaps one of the few large social groups in America to live outside this world of technology. Most Amish don't know what a website looks like. When the weekly Amish newspaper, the *Budget,* published in Sugarcreek, Ohio, announced it wanted to start moving material online, there was a rebellion among its "scribes," 843 reporters who handwrite and send in letters about news in their locales each week. Publisher Keith Rathbun says the concern was "privacy—uncertainty about the Internet."[25]

Arianna Huffington, editor of the *Huffington Post,* once encouraged her guests at a *HuffPost* party to "live blog their experiences during the party." One of the most extensive networks of blogs is political, followed by lesbian-gay-bisexual blogs. But the mommy blogs and the pet blogs are not far behind. Check out *Pets Who Want to Kill Themselves* (http://www. petswhowantokillthemselves.com), whose creator got signed to a book deal two months after he started this blog. Publishers admit they pay close attention to bloggers, which is how the book *I Can Has Cheezburger?* was discovered and went on to sell 100,000 copies.

Then there are the photoblogs that display snapshots of street fashions or street denizens the blogs full of videos, blogs about music, the arts, and sports, "blawgs" about the law, and blogs about the environment, the weather, and even the traffic. You can get advice about selling your house and read nasty comments about other people's real estate on blogs like socketsit.com, or laugh at Wall Street at *Leveraged Sell-Out.* Foodie bloggers can comment on the restaurants they've eaten in (go to *Yelp* to post your review), film bloggers on the movies they've just seen, fashionista bloggers on the stores they've just shopped in. Bloggers like these can do considerable damage if they were unhappy about anything at these venues, and employees who've been laid off in the Great Recession tend to blog about it, to their former employers' chagrin.

Nancy Sinatra maintains a blog about her father at *Sinatra Family,* that lets readers download their favorite Frank Sinatra songs. The *Huffington Post* and the *Daily Kos* are basically blogs, and so are popular social media sites like Facebook and YouTube as well as Twitter, technically a microblog with its 140-character limit on messaging. Even media hotshot Tina Brown, former editor of the *New Yorker* and *Vanity Fair,* has given up on print and started her own blogging website, the *Daily Beast* (http://www.thedailybeast.com), to cover the news and blog about life in the 21st century (a late 2010 merger with *Newsweek* has also made her editor of that news magazine). Newspapers, reading the writing on the computer screen, are increasingly posting to the web and starting their own blogs, assigned to their regular reporters.

These days, even novels and mystery and detective fiction may routinely include blogging as part of the narrative, sometimes centering the whole story on a blogging episode or describing the blogosphere as if setting a scene. Bloggers stepped up to support Susan Boyle on *Britain's Got Talent,* and even though she didn't win, loyal bloggers continue to root for her career. Her success is evidence that the new world of the blogosphere can unearth many creative and talented unknowns. There are bloggers in the bleachers at major sports events, sometimes a source of controversy in their reporting, videos, and not-always-flattering opinion pieces about the games (but "you can't do play-by-play in a blog," one editor says. "You can't type that fast, for crying out loud"). And there are bloggers in the front row at fashion shows doing live blogs sitting next to *Vogue* editor Anna Wintour and scooping her magazine, which won't be printing and publishing the runway news until months later. When 13-year-old blogger Tavi Gevinson, getting famous for her *Style Rookie* blog, crashed the Spring 2010 collections show in Bryant Park, *Vogue* rival *Harper's Bazaar* published her review of the show.

The blog search engine, Technorati, ranked the *Huffington Post* number one among the "100 Top Blogs" in 2010, followed by (2) *TechCrunch,* (3) *TMZ,* (4) *Mashable,* (5) *Engaget,* (6) *Think Progress,* (7) *Boing Boing* (8) the *Daily Beast,* (9) *Buzz Feed,* and (10) *Hot Air.*[26] *Time* magazine doesn't rank its list of the "25 Best Blogs of 2010" but does include *TechCrunch, Gawker,* and *Boing Boing* as "Essential Blogs" (*Mashable* and the *Daily Kos* were given an "Overrated" ranking).[27]

Arianna Huffington told Technorati in a 2009 interview that "it was the excitement of seeing the conversation moving online" (and reading Matt Drudge's *Drudge Report*) that got her into blogging. "The key thing was the interactivity," she says, talking about her first blog, *Arianna Online,* started in the late 1990s. She says she launched the *Huffington Post* in 2005 by just e-mailing "all the interesting people I knew," ending up with 500 people with passwords who could post "when they wanted." By mid-2010, the *Huffington Post* was racking up 24.3 million unique visitors a month and had a staff of 88 editorial staffers, plus 6,000 unpaid bloggers. "Self-expression is the new entertainment," Huffington says. "People don't want to just consume information, they want to participate. Recognizing that impulse is the future of journalism."[28]

The new kid on the blog block is Tumblr, a blogging service that describes itself as "a space in between Twitter and Facebook," according to Mark Coatley, newly hired from *Newsweek* and the site's self-described "media evangelist." Essentially a microblogging site, Tumblr invites users to write more conversationally than they can on Twitter and to post photos, videos, audio, and text, which can be grouped thematically. There's no tracking of followers, but users can send their posts to Twitter and Facebook from Tumblr, which says its purpose is to provide a "web publishing service." It had reached a milestone of one billion posts in August 2010 and collected 7.2 million users, including media like the *Atlantic,* the *New York Times,* and *Forbes.*[29]

WHO READS THIS STUFF ANYWAY?

The Pew Research Center's Internet and American Life Project found that 33 percent of Americans on the Internet say they read blogs, about 24 percent of all U.S. adults, with 11 percent of Internet users reading blogs on a typical day. Only 12 percent of Internet users write blogs, just 5 percent of all adults. Fourteen percent of teens ages 12 to 17 say they write blogs. But blogging is declining among those under 30, another Pew study found, with three-quarters of online teens on social media networks instead.[30]

Those already committed to a blog network show different numbers, however. A 2010 BlogHer network study, "Social Media Matters," surveying its mostly female membership, found that 96 percent of them said they visited blogs weekly. "Blogs are still where substantive conversations are happening," BlogHer chief operating officer Elisa Camahort says. "It's not on Facebook." The survey found that 30 percent of the 18- to 29-year-old women on BlogHer were reading blogs, with 40 percent writing them. Twenty-nine percent of the women ages 26 to 42 were reading blogs, with 28 percent writing them. The numbers drop to 23 percent for boomer blog readers ages 43 to 61, with 18.7 percent of them writing blogs. Only

17 percent of BlogHer users over age 62 were reading blogs, with just 12.6 percent writing a blog. Eighty-one percent of BlogHer bloggers said they write their blogs for self-expression, with 63 percent saying they would go to a blog over social media for advice and purchase recommendations. One-third of BlogHer network users are ages 26 to 42, affluent, and well educated.[31]

Journalists at traditional news outlets can't afford not to read blogs these days. Indeed, the British Broadcasting Corporation (BBC) issued a memo to its reporters requiring that they use social media and blogs for their research.[32] Politicians and government officials read blogs; CEOs of Dow Industrial companies read blogs; and so do movie directors, celebrities, and White House staffers.

One of the biggest lures for readers are gossip blogs like *Gawker,* which dishes with a snarky but all-knowing attitude about the parties and celebrities of the moment, along with who made a fool of himself last night, which celebrity filed for a protection order, and who's running around with whom. It's the kind of minutiae that sustains many blogs in this 24/7 always-on society. When White House chief of staff Rahm Emanuel was sighted at a Washington, D.C., ATM in the Safeway store, it was deemed worth posting. The *New York Times* calls the growing cohort of gossip bloggers "the Walter Winchells of Cyberspace," noting that "the lines between 'reporter' and 'blogger,' 'gossip' and 'news' have blurred almost beyond distinction." Blogging is "now a career path in its own right, offering visibility, influence and an actual paycheck."[33] Emerging gossip bloggers, most still in their twenties, are carving a huge niche for themselves out of the Page Six and Liz Smith print kingdoms.

The best way to get people to read your blog is to stir up some controversy, drawing in people from all sides of an argument, as Bill Wasik documents in his book, *And Then There's This.* He describes his own efforts one summer to win a *Huffington Post* contest, the "Contagious Festival," in which the blog website that got the most hits, or visitors, would win $2,500. Wasik managed to win the contest by posting "The Right-Wing *New York Times,*" which contained joke news leads and headlines guaranteed to tick off conservatives and liberals alike. It became a meme, or oft-linked-to, pass-along cache of information, and was getting 8,000 visits an hour at its peak. "Fascinated by how culture spreads," and thrilled at being a "meme-maker," Wasik points out that his experience shows how you can start trends and affect culture, even in the circus of the Internet.[34]

BLOGGING FOR BUCKS

Bloggers, most of them anyway, are not getting paid to do what they do. But the lure of blogging, beyond personal expression and the satisfactions of having an audience, is that it can sometimes lead to monetary rewards. Corporations have professionals blogging away about their products and are ever-alert to the amateur "influencer" who is doing the same and might be hired, either to blog regularly about a product or to endorse one and talk about it. People writing parenting blogs and beauty blogs have been particularly ripe fodder for the corporate mill. Such arrangements have attracted the eye of the Federal Trade Commission (FTC), which is interested in the product giveaways and payments for endorsements of products.

Many bloggers begin their blogs with the hope of attracting corporate interest, but only about 1 percent of American adults are making some income from a blog, about 1.7 million. But Technorati also reports that 452,000 of those who used blogging as their primary source of income in 2009 earned on average $61,437.20 as self-employed bloggers, more if they were blogging for a corporation. This doesn't include an average investment in the blog of about $10,518 a year, which could include hosting fees, marketing and advertising, and, perhaps, staff. A blogger can make considerably more if he or she is blogging for a corporation, though still most likely will be regarded as a freelancer without benefits. Recruiting advertising for a blog, using an ad network or blog ad network, is a good way to sustain it but not particularly easy to do for the self-employed.[35] Blogging about your own business can raise its profile, certainly, especially if you also alert your followers on Twitter to read your blog.

Publishers keep abreast of blogs to discover new publishing directions and talent, and many bloggers begin with the hope of attracting such attention. The blogosphere has also made it easier than ever before to publish your book yourself. Bowker, publisher of *Books in Print,* reported that for the first time, more print-on-demand (POD) self-published books were published than conventional titles in 2008.[36] One online approach to getting published is to blog (or tweet) your crazy idea and let your audience contribute the content. For example, it took only two months for the author of the blog *Pets Who Want to Kill Themselves,* Duncan Birmingham, to get his readers to send him enough photographs and commentary to sell it all as a book to Three Rivers Press.[37] Professional journalists, many of them newly unemployed or newly rehired by media websites, have taken to the blogosphere in great numbers, finding their own voices and producing some of the most readable and interesting posts. There are pitfalls, however, as *Washington Post* blogger David Weigel discovered when off-the-cuff remarks he made on *Journolist* about Matt Drudge (he "should set himself on fire") leaked out, to the dismay of his employer (Weigel subsequently resigned and now is at *Slate*).[38]

At the White House, blogging is not an officially sanctioned activity, but plenty of websites, bloggers, and Twitterers outside the gates are chronicling every tidbit of minutiae that can be gleaned about the Obamas, the White House staff, and even the family dog. Ana Marie Cox, founder of Wonkette, a website that started chronicling insider Washington politics five years ago, says she started it "as a joke to treat official Washington as a celebrity culture," but now "the joke has turned real.[39] These days, Ms. Cox herself Twitters and blogs about the White House for Air America.

WHO LET THE BLOGS OUT?

Biz Stone, one of the founders of Twitter, chose this clever title for his 2004 book about blogs. In his words, blogs are "the true democratization of the web," "a low barrier of entry to publishing that gives everyone a voice." "I was a blog freak," he says, chronicling his own progress into the field. In his book, Stone describes the early forerunners and inventors who made blogging possible, including Ted Nelson, who coined the term *hypertext* for an idea he had about handling text online, and Tim Berners-Lee, who built on the idea to create a "global hypertext system" he called the World Wide Web.[40]

The word *blog* is a hybrid, evolving as a short form of *web log,* which was how this whole thing got started. *Web log* was the name that programmer Jorn Barger gave in 1997 to the online record he started posting as his daily diary. He named his postings *Robot Wisdom WebLog,* capitalizing *Log* because, he said, "the syllable 'blog' seemed so hideous." Barger was not the first blogger, as other experimental sites along the same lines had been launched earlier, but the *WebLog* name stuck and, despite the capitalized L, morphed into the term for all else that followed.[41] Blogging didn't really begin until 1999, Stone says, with pioneers like Dave Winer. Then Evan Williams with Pyra Labs sparked the blogging revolution with the creation of the website Blogger, which offered free hosting and templates. It was, Stone says, "ground zero for the blogging revolution."[42] Eventually, in 2003, Blogger was acquired by Google.

Like gossip, blogs and blogging are word of mouth, saying things in public that normally would be kept private or undercover or behind someone's back. Like the Internet, the blogosphere is not regulated, so things can be said—and are said—that you won't read anywhere else (libel laws, nonetheless, still apply). Many bloggers are amateur journalists with an admitted axe to grind. And there is plenty of bias, bad spelling, and baloney in much of the blogosphere. Yet it must be said that blogs fulfill the promise of the Internet in opening up the world of information to all. Blogging makes room for anyone who so chooses—the average Joe or Jane or tabloid celebrity—to take a stand, write about it, and publish it.

As a kind of word of mouth, of conversation, blogs also tend to provide a candid, behind-the-scenes look at national events and issues. An official line from the government about sending troops to Afghanistan or proposing health care reform is usually hedged with the boilerplate justifying an official point of view. Blogs, on the other hand, read between the lines of such rhetoric, providing a candid look at what's really going on or how people outside the circle of policy makers read the situation. As blogger Ken Layne famously warned a British foreign correspondent whose report he found faulty, "We can fact check your ass," a war cry that resonated throughout the blogosphere.[43] Like gossip, a blog can spread rumors, but it can also tell the truth to power because no one is stopping it or editing it. There are no gatekeepers in the blogosphere. Just bloggers keeping track.

But there are some basic components, according to Stone, who lists three:

- Chronology, which emphasizes the blog's connection to timeliness, the present moment, the now. Blog posts are arranged in reverse chronology, the newest on top, assuring "freshness," as Stone says. "A blogger is only as good as his or her last post."
- Frequency; that is, a blog needs to be updated constantly to keep its audience.
- Focus on a specific topic or a personality (the author's usually). The voice of a blog is its biggest attraction.[44]

BLOGGERATI: WHO ARE THESE PEOPLE?

Reliable statistics about the Internet are hard to come by and quickly out of date. At last count, there were 500 million active Facebook users, compared to approximately 159 million blogs. According to a Pew Internet study in 2010, 78 percent of Americans use the Internet, with 65 percent of them on broadband at home.[45] What is most interesting about these numbers are the demographics. In its "State of the Blogosphere 2010" report, Technorati found that those who are blogging in the United States are two-thirds male. Sixty-five percent of bloggers are between the ages of 18 and 44 (over half the adult Internet population is 18 to 44 years old). They tend to be well educated: Three out of four, or 79 percent, of those blogging are college graduates, and 43 percent of these have graduate degrees. The majority of bloggers tend to be more affluent than the general U.S. population. One in three has an average annual income of $75,000, while one in four as much as $100,000. Eleven percent say blogging is their primary income source.[46] Blogging is, of course, global, on six continents and in 66 countries at last count, as Technorati found in its 2009 "State of the Blogosphere" survey, with English and Spanish as the most universal blog languages (Japanese and Chinese are next).

"A global culture is in the making" because of bloggers and their readers, as *Born Digital* authors John Palfrey and Urs Gasser assert. And, they say, blogging and the Internet allow in their remixes and mashups of cultures the kind of interaction, like sampling music, that "affects how cultures develop and are understood."[47]

AMERICA, ONLINE

At last count, at least 76 percent of Americans owned a computer, nearly half of them using the Internet each day, joining 1.9 billion other users around the globe. Sixty-five percent of adults in the United States have broadband at home, but about 19 percent of online Americans access the Internet more often on a cell phone or other mobile device than on a computer, a percentage that is growing fast.[48] Personal computer sales are declining, and computer makers like Dell and HP are ramping up efforts to revamp their systems for cloud computing and mobile devices.

Part of the attraction of blogging and reading blogs is simple human curiosity, sticking your nose into someone else's business. The urge for self-expression is another big attraction blogs have. And the opportunity to recreate yourself online is very seductive. In this regard, Cindy Sherman and other artists led the way in assuming masks and personae. The Internet is indeed "a culture of simulation," as media critic Sherry Turkle has said.[49]

Blogs, as Aaron Barlow points out in *Blogging America,* "re-establish the public sphere" just as "coffeehouses, salons, broadsheets, and pamphlets first established it three hundred years ago."[50] Blogs are like speech, with the informality and immediacy of conversation, and they have an audience, real or imagined, listening. What's going on in the culture as a result of blogs is that ideas and influences are arising from this audience rather than being dictated from above, as was the case when culture was defined as high culture versus low culture. In the past, as democracy and free speech opened up the public sphere and as it became cheaper to produce books, plays, music, and, eventually, movies, the populace was awakened to make its own demands and create its own culture. Blogs today offer new avenues of this cultural expression and make new connections among groups, without filters, fees, or gatekeepers. At this point, no one is predicting the demise of blogs or their future, though many blogs are morphing into websites and social media, and Technorati reported that some 95 percent of blogs that are begun are abandoned.[51]

Blogging is, after all, a highly subjective operation, and that may be the point for many bloggers and those who follow them. Information offered in abundance can be hard to distinguish from propaganda, and blogging indulges a blogger's own biases, which seep in easily. One critic warns that our culture is suffering from the superficial, unedited, and opinionated flow of online information that blogging promulgates. Andrew Keen in his book, *The Cult of the Amateur,* says this is what happens "when ignorance meets egoism meets bad taste meets mob rule." What's being blurred, he says, is the line "between fact and opinion, informed expertise and amateurish speculation."[52] Celebrating the amateur over the expert, online discussions are full of misinformation and rumor. Anonymity complicates the picture, and issues of ownership and copyright are rife.

Nonetheless, blogs satisfy a basic human desire for self-expression and, at the same time, the basic human desire to be heard, to have an audience. In this regard, blogs are not the new kids on the block, just a 21st-century version of the 18th-century coffeehouse conversations or, going back earlier, the drawings of cavemen on the walls of ancient caves like Lascaux. In our time, blogs are a medium for the masses, giving voice to countless of the previously unheard and to microcultures of news, politics, business, and opinion.

FOUR

Twitter World

In the absence of telephone or cell phone access or even electricity, Haitians in the ruins of their country after the biggest earthquake in 200 years were using Twitter, the 140-character messaging site, to reach the outside world. At the same time, in China, a torrent of tweets from Chinese citizens able to duck under government censorship responded to Google's threat to pull out of China because of cyberattacks on its computer systems, begging it not to leave. More recently, less than an hour after the massive Japanese earthquake in March 2011, the number of tweets out of Tokyo was over a thousand a minute to tell the world what was happening while power outages crippled other communication systems.[1]

No one could have predicted that Twitter, that oddball idea of a social network, would have become a global safety net, let alone a hugely popular daily communication tool for millions of Twitterati, the people, corporations, and small businesses that have found it a simple way to get their message out. The 140-character messaging site, introduced only in 2006, now has more than 200 million users a month posting 140 million tweets a day. That's 1,600 tweets per second, with an average of 460,000 new accounts per day every month worldwide and counting. According to Nielsen, Twitter has seen more than a 200 percent increase in one year in 2010.[2] Folks were tweeting 5,000 times a day in 2007. By 2008, that number was 300,000, and by 2009 it had grown to 2.5 million per day. Tweets grew 1,400 percent last year to 35 million per day.[3] Even the Dalai Lama is on Twitter. So is Hugh Hefner.

According to a 2010 survey by the Pew Research Center's Internet and American Life Project, 24 percent of adult Internet users were on Twitter in 2010, up from 6 percent in the previous Pew survey in 2008. Pew found major Twitter users in three groups:

- **Young adults:** Internet users ages 18–29 are significantly more likely to use Twitter than older adults.
- **African Americans and Latinos:** Minority Internet users are more than twice as likely to use Twitter as are white Internet users.
- **Urbanites:** Urban residents are roughly twice as likely to use Twitter as rural dwellers.[4]

Reports of the death of Twitter have, obviously, been greatly exaggerated. People are embracing Twitter in a huge way, partly because it is a free and easy way to send a message and partly because Twitter creates an instant audience to read and listen to them. The feedback is instantaneous. It's a giant chat room where you can connect with your friends and followers, letting them know "What's happening?," as Twitter asks, all day and all night long. It's a public display of connections, where you can showcase yourself and your enterprises as much as possible and as you would like to be seen ("This morning I had a toasted bagel and took the dog out for a walk"). The 140-character limit is a challenge, like a puzzle. And there is the instant gratification of sending out hourly bulletins about what you are doing at any given moment and accruing followers, those who sign on to get your messages. "Just like high school," as *Vanity Fair* writer Vanessa Grigoriadis comments, "Twitter is an enormous popularity contest."[5]

That's the major draw, collecting followers who will read your tweets. The more followers you have, the more status in the Twitter world or, as some call it, the statusphere. Number 1 on Twitter in 2011 is Lady Gaga with more than 9,130,986 of her "Little Monsters" as followers (she is also top on Facebook as the first ever to have 10 million friends). On Twitter, as of April 1, 2011, Lady Gaga beat out Justin Bieber (at number 2, with 8,500,907 followers), Britney Spears (number 3, with 7,289,958 followers), and President Barack Obama (number 4, with 7,223,645 followers).[6]

TWEET TIME WITH MARTHA

Martha Stewart had 2,135,912 followers on Twitter by Spring 2011, way ahead of the count for the White House and the NFL. Martha loves to tweet: "It's like a puzzle, 140 characters. I post recipes—'1 c sug'—

photos, news, household tips." Twitter is "a very good informational way" to connect, she says. "I'm a teacher, not a preacher."

Tweeting is "a way to teach," and so is Martha's daily blog, where you might learn "how a horse is shod, how a dog is groomed, how cross-country skiing works," along with getting advice on organizing your house, getting ready for a party, and shopping at a farmer's market. Her goal: to make "the act of homekeeping more interesting and more pleasurable, rather than a drag."

Her company, Martha Stewart Living Omnimedia, has more than 600 employees, with magazines, books, television and radio shows (Martha live-blogs on satellite radio), and websites, along with a product line sold at Macy's and Home Depot—plenty for a "domestic diva" like Martha Stewart to tweet about. *AdAge* has named her one of "10 Marketers Who Transformed American Culture," calling her "an iconic image of female entrepreneurship."

Author's personal interview with Martha Stewart at her home, Cantitoe, in Katonah, New York, January 18, 2010. *On Twitter:* http://www.twitter.com/marthastewart *Blog:* http://www.themarthablog.com

There were at last count 366 Twitter accounts with over a million followers. But 93.6 percent of Twitter users have fewer than 100 followers, and 21 percent have never posted a tweet.[7] Among the Twitterati interviewed by Grigoriadis for her *Vanity Fair* article, several (the article calls them "twilebrities") have amassed more than 1.5 million followers each, putting them among the high-count Twitterati. The women in the magazine article are freelance journalists, marketers, and publicists, busy making a name for themselves if not a career out of constant posts on their Twitter accounts. The age of overshare indeed.

While attention junkies get their fix on Twitter, so do public relations agencies, marketers, and retailers who have discovered the commercial value of posting and building an audience of followers. Celebrities and politicians flock to Twitter, though much of the actual posting may be done by their staff and their interns. Even characters out of the movies and animated figures have Twitter accounts, kept going by overzealous public relations departments. And machine bots do much of the work of posting. A study by Sysomos found that about a quarter of all tweets were being generated by machine, at a rate of about 150 tweets a day. "Of the most active Twitter users updating more than 150 times/day, nearly all of them are bots operated by sources such as hotels offering deals, regional and national news services, regional weather services, the top news within Digg, games, animation services, tags within del.icio.us and financial aggregators. These very active bots account for one-quarter of all tweets."[8]

American business has jumped wholeheartedly into Twitter, recognizing its value as a way to connect with consumers and, especially, a way to measure the market for its products. Realizing this, Twitter management has, as it announces on its website blog, "redesigned its home page to focus on news, trends, and cross-cultural sharing, none of which were originally envisioned," but "this is how people are using the service."[9]

Ashton Kutcher, now sixth on Twitter with 6,509,811 followers, says that the big draw of Twitter is that it has removed the filters between celebrities and fans, big media companies and their customers, so ordinary people can connect with whomever they wish.[10] As with blogs, on Twitter there are essentially no gatekeepers, no editors, no oversight. This frees the Twitterati to say just about anything they want, spawning creativity but also resulting in a lot of trivial and boring information.

According to Website-Monitoring.com in 2010, most Twitter users (45 percent) were 18 to 34 years old. Twenty-four percent of Twitterati were 35 to 49 years old, and 14 percent were 50 years and up, with 14 percent ages 13 to 17. Sixty-nine percent were Caucasian, with 16 percent African American, 11 percent Hispanic, and 3 percent Asian. The survey showed 53 percent of Twitter users have no children. Fifty-one percent are college graduates and graduate degree holders.[11]

The majority of Twitterati are women (55 percent). And a study done at Harvard Business School showed that women on Twitter are 25 percent more likely to follow a man than a woman; men have 15 percent more followers on Twitter, and they are more than twice as likely to follow other men.[12] Just 5 percent of active users generate more than 75 percent of updates and activity.[13] Most Twitterati are in cities, New York City specifically, followed by Los Angeles and Toronto, Canada, and then San Francisco and Boston (the city with the most new users in 2009 was Detroit). A Pew Internet survey found that Twitterati tend to be well educated, but most are earning only between $30,000 and $60,000, perhaps because of the age demographic.[14] The Sysomos survey found that the more followers you have on Twitter, the more you will tend to tweet. And those who are active on social-networking sites like Facebook are also more likely to use Twitter.[15] In a sense, access to the Internet and Twitter is an elitist activity, leaving out anyone who doesn't have a computer or mobile device and those who have not embraced the digital world at all, including the older generation.

HOME TWEET HOME

Twittering is easy, and it's free. As with other social media, you simply sign up, post a profile, and log in. On your home page, there's just a box with a question: "What's happening?" (when Twitter first started, the question was "What are you doing?") You put in your 140-character answer (about 15 words, more or less, with some of the same kind of shorthand texters use), and there it is for your followers and all the world to see. What you tweet on your page is public and it stays there, at least up to 3,200 posts, when it will be archived (92 percent of Twitterati leave their posts public). Now your posts will be in the Library of Congress, too, which has archived the entire Twitter site of posts, searchable on Google. Only a direct message, between you and a follower, is private, and Twitter sends these to your email account.

In posting a tweet, you can "retweet" some interesting information, links, or comments by someone else that you've read on one of the pages you're following. You just have to credit it. For example, "RT @Martha Stewart: cupcakes made easy http://marthastewart.com." The trick is to get your message plus the retweet source information into 140 characters, possibly by shortening the character count for the actual message to 125 or using one of the websites that shortens your URLs, for example, bit. ly.com. Twitter has added a new "Tweet" button that virtually eliminates retweeting anything, automatically posting it.

Using a hashtag, which is a keyword with a "hash" or pound sign in front of it like this—#haiti—gets you into any ongoing discussion about that topic. You can also check the "Trending" list on the right-hand menu, and pick up on any of those topics the same way, with a hashtag (#Obama, #Sarah Palin, etc.). In the blizzards of 2010, the hashtag was #snowverkill ("PLEASE buy boots maybe then it won't snow anymore.")

Twitter comes in six languages so far: English, French, German, Spanish, Italian, and Japanese, and it is available on cell phones in at least 26 countries. Many countries have started their own Twitter copycat sites, like China, which has blocked out Twitter and launched several of its own Twitter-like sites (which the government can monitor and which are always, it seems, "down for maintenance"—read undergoing surveillance operations).

"Last tweet?"

TWITTER APPS

Twitter users themselves have adapted the site to make it more user-friendly in ways, as the company itself says, "we couldn't have imagined." "Platforms evolve," and the Twitterati came up with the retweet—"a great example of Twitter teaching us what it wants to be," cofounder Biz Stone says[16]—and the hashtag to enhance the grouping of messages. Twitter itself added "trending topics" and a search bar, and it has introduced @earlybird to allow brands to broadcast special limited-time deals. Twitter is also adding "Twitter Places" to let tweeters tag their posts with their location and tell followers where they are. Businesses quickly saw the opportunity to collect tweets from people in line at the movies, shops, or concerts. A website, PleaseRobMe.com, started monitoring social media location sites to show that while people might leave the lights on when they go away, they are still letting the world know they are not home, via the Internet.

New from Twitter itself is a "Tweet" button that users can embed on their sites to allow sharing across platforms and make the "Retweet" button obsolete. The company claims that the chance to gather more personal data, as Facebook's "Like" button does, did not motivate the new feature.

Twitter will now allow "promoted tweets" that ad companies can buy to appear on "selected searches." Multiple third-party applications have been launched, too many to count, and enough so that Twitter is limiting access times. Top apps like Twitpik allow users to post photos, TweetDeck lets them group their incoming messages, and Twitaholic lists rankings according to the number of followers.[17]

TWEETING FOR DOLLARS

A survey by the University of Southern California Center for the Digital Future (CDF) in July 2010 revealed that virtually no Twitter user would pay for Twitter if the site put up a paywall. "Twitter has no plans to charge its users, but this result illustrates, beyond any doubt, the tremendous problem of transforming free users into paying users," CDF Director Jeffrey Cole said in a statement. "Online providers face major challenges to get customers to pay for services they now receive for free."[18]

Twitter is word of mouth, a real-time collection of people's ideas and comments that is a gold mine for business and corporations to gauge customer reactions. It's better than an exit poll to find out what people are thinking and to keep a brand in the public consciousness. You can promote your business, announce company news, and, most important, keep a close eye on consumer sentiment and preferences about your brand.

No one has figured out yet how to make a profit by being a heavy user, nor how to make Twitter itself profitable, though search deals with Google and Microsoft's Bing have helped, and Twitter will begin selling ads on its own search and some apps. This doesn't seem to bother Twitterati or the site founders. That would be Biz Stone, Evan Williams, and Jack Dorsey, who launched it in August 2006, using web forms like instant messaging and text messaging.

HOW TWITTER GOT STARTED

The idea was that if it's free, people will come, the concept behind Facebook and other start-up social media sites. According to Twitter, the site began because Jack Dorsey wanted a easy, simple way to find out what his friends were doing.[19] Twitter was funded initially by Obvious, a creative environment in San Francisco, California. The first prototype was built in two weeks in March 2006 and launched publicly in August 2006.

The service grew in popularity very quickly, and in May 2007, it became Twitter, Inc.[20]

Where did the name Twitter come from? Dorsey, who kept a diary about starting Twitter, explains it:

> We wanted to capture that feeling: the physical sensation that you're buzzing your friend's pocket. It's like buzzing all over the world. So we did a bunch of name-storming, and we came up with the word "twitch," because the phone kind of vibrates when it moves. But "twitch" is not a good product name because it doesn't bring up the right imagery. So we looked in the dictionary for words around it, and we came across the word "twitter," and it was just perfect. The definition was "a short burst of inconsequential information," and "chirps from birds." And that's exactly what the product was.

The whole bird thing: bird chirps sound meaningless to us, but meaning is applied by other birds. The same is true of Twitter: a lot of messages can be seen as completely useless and meaningless, but it's entirely dependent on the recipient. So we just fell in love with the word. It was like, "Oh, this is it." We can use it as a verb, as a noun, it fits with so many other words. If you get too many messages you're "twitterpated"—the name was just perfect.[21] The initial inspiration for a messaging site like Twitter, Dorsey says, was the dispatch system used by emergency and transportation services, bike messengers, and truck couriers to track their whereabouts. Taxicabs were using GPS, CB radio, and cell phones.

Transposing that concept involved SMS (short messaging service) to make texting available by phone. As Dorsey explained, "SMS allowed this other constraint, where most basic phones are limited to 160 characters before they split the messages. So in order to minimize the hassle and thinking around receiving a message, we wanted to make sure that we were not splitting any messages. So we took 20 characters for the user name, and left 140 for the content. That's where it all came from."[22] And that's what made Twitter a ready-made messaging site for cell phones, BlackBerries, iPhones, and more. No one is tied to a computer to use it; it is as portable as any mobile device, a key component in its success.

At first, Twitter appealed mainly to techies. Nobody else really noticed it much until November 2008 when a terrorist takeover of fancy hotels in Mumbai flooded the site with tweets about what was happening, way ahead of any news bureau reports. Ten Pakistani terrorists were storming the city, taking hostages in two hotels, the Taj Mahal and Oberi Trident, and fanning out to other locations using bombs, grenades, and guns. In all, 175 people, including nine of the attackers, were killed, and 308 were injured.[23] The television feed to the hotels was shut down because the terrorists were using it. Victims trapped in the hotels commandeered by the terrorists tweeted for help on their cell phones and relayed minute-by-minute reports. "At the peak of the violence," the *New York Times* reported, "more than one message per second with the word 'Mumbai' in it was being posted onto Twitter."[24] As Twitter became the communication mode of choice, the Indian government tried to block it. By the time news organizations got there, the crisis had passed, and the nonjournalists on Twitter had done their job of informing the world of what was happening.

This was just the beginning of Twitter's role as an advance alert system. Since then, it has been the crucial communication tool for Japanese caught in an earthquake and tsunami in March 2011, protesters in Egypt and Libya in 2011, in the June 2009 Iranian election protests, the 2010 celebrations of the Islamic Republic in Iran, and more. Twitterati were also the first responders in the miracle on the Hudson plane landing and the Haitian earthquake. In the Iranian election crisis, the U.S. State Department asked Twitter to put off its scheduled shutdown for maintenance to keep it going for protesters, and Twitter complied.

Governments are threatened by Twitter, which proves its populist appeal, and so try to shut it down. The Egyptian government under Mubarak successfully shut down Twitter and other social media in January 2011 (but not soon enough to keep protesters from organizing). In the 2010 protest activity during Iran's anniversary celebrations, the Iranian government blocked Gmail, shut down text-messaging service, and slowed down the Internet, saying it would start its own e-mail service instead. In China, where the Internet Police force is 30,000 strong, a Google shutdown succeeded after hackers, probably employed by the government, broke into the service.

Twitter itself was shut down for nearly a whole day in August 2009 when hackers deluged the website with junk tweets (they attacked Google and Facebook as well). None of Twitter's regular users could access the site; instead, they got spam e-mails. The reaction from Twitterati was intense, showing how much they had come to rely on the service. In fact, early in its existence, Twitter did have unexpected downtimes, and a graphic picturing red birds hoisting a whale from the ocean, labeled the "fail whale" by users, showed up on-screen to signal that the service was down. Twitter also shut down temporarily in the summer of 2009 when Michael Jackson died and the number of tweets doubled as users tried to get information.

The "fail whale" couldn't keep up. Google Search was also briefly over-whelmed, and the gossip site *TMZ* had numerous interruptions.

Nonjournalists on the scene sending out real-time dispatches beat news organizations every time, which is why the BBC recently issued an all-points bulletin to its news staff telling them to check social media regu-larly, a major shift for a hidebound company that has scorned nonjournalist sources. "Today content is passed on in social media by the audience and that has real credibility," BBC World Service Director Peter Horrocks says. "Social media provides journalists with a wider range of opinion, and gives them access to a whole range of voices. ... It is a faster medium. ... It shouldn't be too difficult to use social media in the same way as live reporting."[25] Certainly the Internet and social media like Twitter and Fa-cebook are a huge challenge to print publications of all kinds, maybe the biggest. Yet only 8 percent of U.S. adults say they trust Twitter as a source, the same percentage as those who trust traditional media, according to a Zogby Interactive survey.[26] Twitter changed its opening question, "What are you doing?" to "a different, more immediate question," "What's hap-pening?" in November 2009, to accommodate its growing relevance to breaking news:

> Sure, someone in San Francisco may be answering "What are you doing?" with "Enjoying an excellent cup of coffee," at this very mo-ment. However, a birds-eye view of Twitter reveals that it's not exclu-sively about these personal musings. Between those cups of coffee, people are witnessing accidents, organizing events, sharing links, breaking news, reporting stuff their dad says, and so much more.

The fundamentally open model of Twitter created a new kind of infor-mation network and it has long outgrown the concept of personal status updates. Twitter helps you share and discover what's happening now among all the things, people, and events you care about. "What are you doing?" isn't the right question anymore—starting today, we've shortened it by two characters. Twitter now asks, "What's happening?" We don't expect this to change how anyone uses Twitter, but maybe it'll make it easier to explain to your dad.[27] Twitter also has a set of rules to rein in the unruly. Though the Twitter website posts no specific policy on foul language, it does rule out "obscene or pornographic images in either your profile picture or user background." You can't impersonate other people or businesses to deceive, publish other people's confidential information like a social security number (without their permission), threaten violence, promote illegal activities, or infringe on trademarks or copyrights. No "user squatting," serial accounts, or spamming either.[28]

TWITTER ENVY

New forms of social media pop up daily, many of them out to capture some of that Twitter charisma. People tend to spend a huge amount of time on Twitter, spurring other social networks to compete. Google has started its own version of Twitter called Buzz, designed on the same model (and Twitter itself has added a Google-style Search button). Google's Buzz is connected to its Gmail service (where you have to have an account to get into Buzz) and works like Twitter with considerably more complexity, off-putting to some users.

Unlike Twitter, there is no prescribed text limit. And it doesn't let you retweet a good post to your followers. You have to go back onto Gmail to do that. But you can post to your Buzz account from Gmail. Twitter and Buzz are connected, but it's a one-way street: You can't post your Buzzes to Twitter, only the other way around. Posts on Buzz are not strictly chronological; if someone responds to a Buzz you posted a week ago, the whole post plus comments goes to the top of the list.

Buzz still has bugs to work out. During its first week, many new users were alarmed to find the names of everyone they customarily e-mailed through Gmail listed as their new followers on Buzz, meaning that not only were friends and family named but also their Botox doctor and secret hook-ups, there for all to see. The outcry meant Google had to fix that fast, and to its credit it did, over a weekend, issuing an apology. Now users can label messages "public" or "private" (but not so for replies to a post). Buzz does let you link to Picasa to post photos, to YouTube and Flickr for video, and to Facebook. And it's easy to get into Buzz from Gmail with a single click.

In its quest to grab a bigger share of social networking and Internet control, Google also plans to introduce an ultrahigh-speed network, something that will allow surfing the web at a gigabit a second, about 100 times faster than most broadband connections. Right now, it's a test run to show it can be done.

Facebook itself is incorporating some Twitter features into its platform, now that its bid to acquire Twitter fell through. With Facebook Lite, users can browse a streamlined, simpler version that shows status updates as Twitter does and can tag names of friends or companies with the @Twitter signal to collect mentions of those names. Facebook and Twitter have some reciprocity: Businesses and celebrities can send status updates to Twitter from Facebook without going on Twitter, and Twitter can send tweets to Facebook.

TWITTER CULTURE

Let's go back to Marshall McLuhan for a minute: "Any technology tends to create a new human environment. Script and papyrus created the social environment we think of in connection with the empires of the ancient world. The stirrup and the wheel created unique environments of enormous scope. ... Printing from movable types created a quite unexpected new environment—it created the PUBLIC."[29] Print," as McLuhan noted, "transformed society from an auditory/oral culture to a visual culture," altering the ratio among our senses. Now, "in our time, the sudden shift from the mechanical technology of the wheel [and print] to the technology of electric circuitry represents one of the major shifts of all historical time."[30]

What would he say about the Internet and Twitter? Certainly these offer a totally "new human environment," one that we ourselves aren't even able to categorize yet. We can certainly mine McLuhan's mantra, "The medium is the message," for clues, maybe even reversing it, in the case of Twitter, to "The message is the medium," where the high volume of social connectivity and interactive messaging has created a brand-new cultural matrix for the exchange of ideas. As a constant stream of real-time information (and, maybe, information overload), Twitter has meant an enormous upswing in up-to-the-minute communication among global populations. The "alchemy of the Web," as one social observer calls it, is giving a mass audience access to culture and engineering social transformation on a larger scale than ever before.[31] But critics of Twitter point to the predominance of the hive mind in such social media, the kind of groupthink that submerges independent thinking in favor of conformity to the group, the collective. *New York Times* columnist David Carr calls this "the throbbing networked intelligence."[32] Others call it dangerous and dumb. People may fear embarrassment or being thought stupid because on Twitter they are performing publicly and in a group. They tend to conform even when they are showing off. Twitter doesn't squelch clever or obscene remarks, but it does exert social pressure and foster an "ambient awareness," as technology guru Clive Thompson calls it.[33]

In her article about Twitter, "I Tweet, Therefore I Am," writer Peggy Orenstein raises a constant concern, asking, "Are Twitter posts an expression of who we are—or are they changing who we are?" viewing her own tweets as "a tacit referendum on who I am, or at least who I believe myself to be." But, she admits, these were "not really about my own impressions: it was about how I imagined—and—wanted others to react to them." The risk is that in a "performance culture," the "packaged self" could erode "the very relationships it purports to create," alienating us "from our own humanity." We need "to sort out the line between person and persona, the public and the private self," Orenstein concludes.[34] A study of the decline of empathy among college students conducted in 2010 by researchers at the University of Michigan reinforces concerns about the pitfalls of spending too much time online with virtual friends.[35]

As a graphic example of what Twitter culture could mean to so-called high culture, a British author offered some tongue-in-cheek versions of classic literature in the 140-character count of Twitter:

Lady Chatterley's Lover by D. H. Lawrence: "Upper-class woman gets it on with gamekeeper."

Waiting for Godot by Samuel Becket: "Vladimir and Estragon stand next to a tree and wait."

Ulysses by James Joyce: "Man walks around Dublin. We follow every minute detail of his day. He's probably overtweeting."

Great Expectations by Charles Dickens: "Orphan given money by secret follower. He thinks it's @misshavisham but it turns out to be @magwitch."

The Catcher in the Rye by J. D. Salinger: "Rich kid thinks everyone is fake except for his little sister. Has breakdown. @markchapman is now following @johnlennon."[36]

Twitter has spawned a number of literary efforts, most notably, *Sh*t My Dad Says* by Justin Halpern, compiling his father's earthy sayings in tweets. Sample tweets: "Tennessee is nice. The first time I vomited was in Tennessee I think." "That woman was sexy … Out of your league? Son. Let women figure out why they won't screw you, don't do it for them."[37] A CBS pilot show, *@\$#*! My Dad Says,* starring William Shatner, began in fall 2010.

Ice Storm author Rick Moody wrote a short story in 153 tweets for the online zine *Electric Literature;* it came out over a three-day period in November 2009. Sample plot and character from the story, "Some Contemporary Characters": "Saw him on OKCupid. Agreed to meet. In his bio he said he had a 'different conception of time.' And guess what? He didn't show."[38]

Now the national mood can even be monitored by surveying Twitter tweets. A team of researchers from the College of Computer and Information Science at Northeastern University and from Harvard Medical School surveyed Twitter service from September 2006 to August 2009 to find out how happy (or sad) Americans are at different times of the day.[39]

They found that during the week, predictably, people are happier before and after work, in the early morning and late evening, something that held true on both the east and west coasts despite the time differences. Weekends were prime-time happy time, peaking on Sunday mornings. The unhappiest time was Thursday evenings. "We're not claiming we've made a great scientific discovery," Sune Lehmann, one of the researchers, said. But "there's great promise in the data."[40]

One Twitter problem, germane to all social media, is that it makes it easy to circulate fake stories and rumors. False news items that have been retweeted include things like "Steve Jobs was rushed to an E.R. following a severe heart attack," "Jeff Goldblum was killed in an accident in New Zealand," and "JetBlue and American Airlines flew doctors to post-earthquake Haiti free of charge." All of these are patently untrue, as Professor Sreenath Sreenvasan of the Columbia University Graduate School of Journalism has noted.[41]

WHY DO THE TWITTERATI TWEET?

It's cool and it's hip to be on Twitter, drinking the Twitter Kool-Aid, whether you tweet much or not (75 percent of tweets are put out by only 5 percent of users). The social cachet is seductive, even if you have few followers. Actually, you need to experience Twitter yourself to understand it. It's fast, it's free, and, it turns out, Twitter is fun. It's full of people younger than you. But the most exciting part of Twitter for its devotees is the instant audience that assembles around your tweets. Even if you have no followers when you start out, they start showing up and a group forms. Suddenly you have your groupies, your loyal fans. Even the White House is into the act, with former Press Secretary Robert Gibbs posting the first tweet in February 2010. A Russian ambassador to NATO couldn't resist either, taking to his Twitter account to respond in harsh terms to a U.S. plan to deploy missile interceptors in Russia.[42] Even the deadly cobra that escaped from the Bronx Zoo in March 2011 had its own Twitter account, #BronxZoosCobra, a spoof, chronicling its every move around town, including visiting the Empire State Building and going to Broadway shows.

Why do people use Twitter? According to Social Media at Work, 50 percent of Twitter users say they use it to update their status (meaning what's happening). About 39 percent say they use it to follow celebrities, and another 39 percent to "stay current." Thirty percent use Twitter to stay in touch with "friends I know."[43]

The amount of banal and trivial postings on Twitter has invited criticism. Pear Analytics, a Texas marketing analysis site, found in an August 2009 survey that more than 40 percent of tweets at the time amounted to what it called "pointless babble," with another 37-plus percent classified as just "conversation." The peak times of day for such tweets were between 2:30 and 3 p.m. on weekdays. Right after lunch, around 2 p.m., "news" (3.6 percent of tweets) and "self-promotion" (5.85 percent) tweets were at their peak. "Pass-along" items or retweets amounted to 8.7 percent of tweets, most at 11:30 in the morning.[44]

As Heather Anderson, the blogger who runs the website Dooce.com, expressed it:

What I mostly find annoying about Twitter is the sensation of hearing tidbits of a hundred people's thoughts zooming past. You know how in movies, they always show that a psychic person is psychic by having them walk through a crowded public place and being bombarded with voices from all the thoughts of all the people around them, and then they wince and hold their head? That's how Twitter feels to me most of the time. It makes me dizzy.[45]

Yet the open forum for self-expression is too much to resist for many active Twitterers. In "Why Twitter Will Endure," media columnist David Carr says, "I've come to understand that the real value of the service is listening to a wired collective voice," a "throbbing networked intelligence."[46] Carr's take: "I'm convinced Twitter is here to stay." But *New Yorker* critic George Packer scoffs, "Twitter is crack for media addicts."[47]

For politicians, celebrities, and corporations, Twitter has made getting the message out much easier and more efficient. President Barack Obama had a Twitter account during the 2008 election, @barack obama, which made connections with the electorate no one else had tried yet in such intensity. Most of the tweets were written by Democratic National Committee staffers, but it did the job. The White House itself has now started tweeting, with former Press Secretary Robert Gibbs leading off on February 16, 2010. His tweet: "Learning about 'the twitter'—easing into this with first tweet—any tips?" Gibbs had collected over 22,500 followers. You can reach the new Press Secretary Jay Carey at jaycareyfacts, but be forewarned: your tweets to him will end up in the federal archives in compliance with the Presidential Records Act.

FIVE

Are Blogs and Twitter Hijacking Journalism?

Newspapers and magazines are folding, print media layoffs are in the thousands, journalists are on suicide watch, and J-school professors say teaching journalism these days feels as if they are teaching history. The ascendancy of blogs and Twitter has struck fear into the hearts of the mainstream media as citizen journalists regularly scoop news outlets on breaking news. All it takes is a tweet on a cell phone to beat traditional journalists still on their way to the scene.

This is a headline issue, debated daily in the pages of newspapers, some on the verge of bankruptcy. As blogs and Twitter and other social networks take over the Internet, a new generation of readers has migrated online for its news. The question of what is going to happen to traditional journalism (even now known as old media) is keeping journalists awake nights and taking up plenty of space in op-ed columns lately. Even the U.S. Senate held hearings about the Internet's impact on news and newspapers. As columnist Frank Rich commented in the *New York Times,* "You know it's bad when the Senate is moved...to weigh in with hearings on 'The Future of Journalism.'"[1]

Like street subcultures, the bloggerati and Twitterati are usurping the codes of conventional news gathering with a new citizen journalism that threatens a huge upheaval in mainstream media. Traditional journalism is definitely on the ropes when even the *Washington Post,* that reliable chronicle of all things political, is "doing a long, slow fade," with its circulation now just two-thirds of what it was a decade ago, a 13 percent decline in sales, a decimated staff, and the last of its domestic bureaus—Chicago, Los Angeles, and New York—shut down.[2]

Is the profession in meltdown? Has a counterculture of Twittering, blogging citizen journalists staked out so much territory on the web that established news sources can't compete? As Michael Hirschorn, writing in the *Atlantic*, put it, these may be the "End Times" (a pun on the possible end of the *New York Times*) as "a digital future heaves into view."[3] Indeed, there is a huge structural shift underway, propelled by technology and the changing behaviors it has given rise to, as an online populace of ordinary people revels in the interactivity and self-expression that the Internet makes possible, colonizing the territory of traditional journalism with news on demand.

The media of the counterculture have already beaten established journalists to the punch on some big stories. The first responses and news of the earthquake and tsunami in Japan in March 2011 were on Twitter (hashtag #hitsunami), not cable news networks. A monster earthquake in Chile knocked out every means of communication except cell phones, on which Twittering citizens sent cries for help and reports of the disaster. Similarly, in Haiti, cell phone tweets emerged first from the rubble of the earthquake there. The "miracle on the Hudson" landing of a bird-stalled jet airplane in the Hudson River in January 2009 was first reported on Twitter, then so new nobody had even heard of it six months earlier. Twitterati also sounded the first alarms about a low-flying 747 Air Force One plane tailed by fighter jets over Lower Manhattan in the spring of 2009 as panicked office workers fearing another 9/11 fled skyscrapers in New Jersey and New York City.

It's happening even as we speak, as each new crisis in government or politics or weather or disaster makes it into the public marketplace at ultrahigh speed. News organizations can't get their people out there fast enough to beat the news feeds already spreading worldwide from on-the-scene citizen reporters. Globally, foreign governments have always tried to censor traditional news media, but now they are threatened with losing complete control of information as citizens flock to the instant and unfiltered Internet. In Iran, a 30th-anniversary celebration fostering disorderly protest exploded on Twitter until the government shut the site down. In China, too, government agencies sensing a loss of control have banned Google, Facebook, and other social media and tried to substitute a homegrown version that Chinese citizens quickly learned to evade.

The explosion of opinion and new voices from the populace now expressed in blogs and on Twitter is changing not only journalism but culture itself, transforming it from the bottom up and opening the world of information to all. With no gatekeeper editors or corporate oversight, the Internet tends to level the playing field and makes an end run around sanctioned and official rhetoric to allow free expression of ideas from often-overlooked segments of the population. Digital media also allow coverage of issues and events seldom covered by traditional news outlets. Now some newsrooms are even basing their coverage on what's popular online, with daily surveys of blogs, Twitter, and social media network traffic and topics.[4]

Critics say that without investigative reporters and journalists accountable to their editors and readers, many political and cultural institutions could suffer and spin out of control (one reporter at the Senate hearings predicted there would be "halcyon days for corrupt politicians" coming up if mainstream journalists were no longer on the job).[5] They say there would be no in-depth coverage of important issues that require thorough consideration, no vetting of political candidates and incumbents beyond the superficial, and no persistent long-term oversight of serious social problems. Television taught people to judge on image, but the Internet is teaching them to go for the jugular and cut to the chase. Forget background and context; short attention spans want it now. It's word of mouth on steroids.

"QUALITY LOCAL NEWS"

One guy who believes in the future of print is James D. Dunning, Jr. He is chairman of the board of Freedom Communications, Inc., an Irvine, California–based media company with 33 daily newspapers nationwide including the influential *Orange County Register,* 77 weekly papers, magazines, eight broadcast stations, and 40 websites.

As former chairman of Ziff Davis Media and of Petersen Publishing and former president of *Rolling Stone,* Dunning has been a big force in print and digital media and television. At Freedom Communications, he says, "I want to focus on being the biggest, best, local provider of what I call the three 'Cs'—content, community, and circulation":

> We're going to capture the local share of the ad market and not just be victims of trends. We will be platform agnostic. Our leverage and advantage is that we have newspapers. I want us to be great and a winner in our space.

The future of journalism? "Local news," Dunning says. "Print is quality local news."

Author's personal interview with James D. Dunning, Jr., September 5, 2010. Website: http://www.freedom.com

Bill Keller, executive editor of the *New York Times,* reviewing a new biography of *Time* magazine founder Henry Luce, comments on the need for professional journalism as "a civic good, in that a democracy needs a shared base of trustworthy information upon which to make its judgments."

> The cacophony of today's media—in which rumor and invective often outpace truth-testing, in which shouting heads drown out sober reflection, in which it is possible for people to feel fully informed without ever encountering an opinion that contradicts their prejudices—plays some role in the polarizing of our politics, the dysfunction of our political system and the increased cynicism of the American electorate.[6]

Arianna Huffington, proprietor of the Huffington Post.com, says people are now getting their news "not on a couch" but on "a galloping horse," on the Internet.[7] By the time the nightly news comes on at 6:30 P.M., anybody who still watches it already knows what happened that day. But columnist Chris Hedges says it appears that "the masses prefer to be entertained rather than informed." He comments, "The decline of print has severed a connection with a reality-based culture, one in which we attempt to make fact the foundation for opinion and debate, and replaced it with a culture in which facts, opinions, lies, and fantasy are interchangeable."[8]

In addition, it seems, the proliferation of opinion that social media offer has tended to radically polarize the population, as people now can find and gravitate to news sites that reflect their own point of view. This is expressed on television, too, especially by cable news stations, which have discovered that ratings rise as they play to the politically like-minded. Ideologies color the newscasts, and the accusations that the press is full of lefties are often acknowledged and encouraged. If the White House leaves Fox News out of its press conferences because of its right-wing reputation, nobody gets upset except right-wing bloggers (although recently Fox News has been given a front seat at White House press conferences). With an electorate so highly polarized, the fights get nasty, and the Tea Party movement has gained ground organizing outraged conservatives. Followers of blogs and Twitter can easily find their views reflected and discussed in any number of ways all day long.

To be fair, other factors threaten traditional news outlets. The economic meltdown of the Great Recession has cut advertising to the bone and sent newspapers and magazines out of business by the dozen, stalwarts like the *Rocky Mountain News,* the *Christian Science Monitor,* and the *Seattle*

Post-Intelligencer among them. The *New York Times* has kept the *Boston Globe* in print despite its near-death experience in 2009. Overall, newspaper revenues in 2009 were down 29 percent. Once the lifeblood of a print newspaper, print advertising fell by 29 percent in the first half of 2009, the greatest quarterly drop since the Great Depression.[9] After all, it turns out to be cheaper to advertise on the Internet and Craigslist than in print.

In their new book *The Death and Life of American Journalism,* authors Robert W. McChesney and John Nichols argue that the problem isn't just the Internet and the economic crisis of 2008. They point out that newspaper circulation has been "trending downward since 1987. Fewer Americans read a daily newspaper today than in 1950, yet the population has more than doubled." "Before the 1970s, people aged 18–30 read daily newspapers at close to the same levels as did older Americans," but "the percentage of under-30 newspaper readers began to fall around that time and was a well-established fact long before the World Wide Web." In the age of the Internet, a 2007 study found that only 16 percent of 18- to 30-year-olds were reading a daily newspaper.[10]

According to a 2009 study by the Pew Research Center's Internet and American Life Project, on a typical day 61 percent of Americans get their news online, with 26 percent accessing it on cell phones, 33 percent of all cell phone users. "News is pocket-size" now, according to the study, and Americans are becoming "news grazers."[11]

Part of the reason for the decline of newspapers, McChesney and Nichols claim, is that "large corporate chains accelerated the long-term trend," gobbling up daily newspapers as family owners sold out; the new owners "were dedicated to maximizing their [profits]." News organizations "ceased to be anything but a business," and a traditional "rich mix" of news gave way to softer coverage including gossip, self-help, weather, and "exercise tips." To media conglomerates, it made no business sense to put in the time and staff to produce complex stories and investigative journalism. The dumbing down of the newspaper gave many readers, including younger ones, no compelling reasons to read one, and as the new century dawned, the Internet began to make inroads on that readership as well. Meanwhile, from 1992 to 2002, McChesney and Nichols say, newsrooms were being decimated as corporate owners pursued profits by cutting staff, in the time-honored corporate way.[12]

The writing was on the wall, in other words, long before the Internet became a major competitor to print media. But the Internet is a powerful reason readers have fled print. It's free, and for content providers, the cost of posting news on a website (much of it "borrowed" from print) is minimal.

But as the world moves to the web, print media are struggling to get there with it, setting up auxiliary websites to post the daily paper (and trying to figure out how to make people pay for it). When the *New York Times* announced it was going to charge for its online edition, there was a huge public outcry. No fair, when most of the Internet is free.

Apple's iPad arrived in the spring of 2010, selling over three million tablets in short order and opening the door for newspapers and magazines to create iPad apps and go online. Since then, Apple has sold 15 million iPads and launched a second version, iPad2. It's easier to read a magazine on the iPad, which opens two pages at once horizontally. *Vanity Fair, Time, Popular Science,* and *Gourmet* (which has returned online after going out of the print business) already have iPad versions, but they're charging by the issue. The *Wall Street Journal,* which has been online for some time, has an iPad app and lets viewers look at the front page and some articles for free but sells subscriptions. The *New York Times* online version could be read on the iPad for free until they set up the paywall in March 2011.

GOING VIRAL

One of the first hints that things might be changing for print media has been the move of the younger generation away from reading a print newspaper. Instead, they are getting all their news online or from more entertaining television personalities like Jon Stewart and Stephen Colbert. And, for the first time, more people of all ages now get news online rather than from newspapers (41% online vs. 31% newspapers),[13] though television news still outranks both as a news source. A Pew Research Center Project for Excellence in Journalism study in 2010 found that online news readers are "grazers," clicking around the web for news wherever they can find it. Two-thirds of them (68 percent) are under age 50, with 29 percent of those under age 30. This entire group of online news readers, which includes whites and some Hispanics, tends to be well educated with incomes tending to be higher than those of American adults in general, with 50 percent employed full-time. Twenty-four percent of this group are single. The study found that 50 percent of African Americans, 38 percent of non-Hispanic whites, and 32 percent of Hispanics tend to get news entirely offline.[14]

What kind of news are they reading? The weather tops everything, according to this study, with 81 percent of online news readers checking weather news most often. Second in line is national news, followed by health news. Offline, television is still the favorite source of news according to 37 percent of these online news readers, followed by portal news aggregators like GoogleNews, AOL, and Topix. Twitter was the least-used news source. Still, online news readers spend only three minutes and four seconds on each news site, more evidence of grazing.

A 2010 survey done by the Center for the Digital Future at the University of Southern California Annenberg School for Communication and Journalism showed that only 56 percent of Americans on the Internet thought newspapers were now an important source of news. Seventy-eight percent of Americans on the Internet said the Internet was an important source, though only half said they thought online news was reliable. Sixty-eight percent said television was still an important source of news.[15] Newspaper subscriptions and newsstand sales started to tank way before the economic meltdown hit, and now they are dropping readers at a rate of 2 percent annually, with a 7.1 percent loss of weekly circulation.[16] It became apparent that new generations were not in the habit of reading the newspaper way back in the 1990s. But it's not all the fault of the Internet; television certainly has had something to do with this decline.

The people still relying on newspapers for news are older, perhaps quite a bit older. It's a lifelong habit for older generations, retrieving the paper off the front steps or picking it up at the newsstand, reading it with morning coffee or on the commuter train (folded a special way so it doesn't take up much room). They are a loyal readership, but they are not being replaced with a younger cohort of print newspaper readers. Yet readership among the older generation has declined as well; only 32 percent of those 30 and above still reach for the daily paper.[17]

What's clear is that trust in newspaper and television news has declined measurably. A 2010 Gallup poll found that only 25 percent of Americans had confidence in these news media, on a par with their lack of confidence in banks and just above their "dismal" trust in health care organizations and big business. It's also clear that "the media as a whole are not gaining new fans as they struggle to serve and compete with growing demand for online news, social media, and mobile platforms," Gallup said.[18]

Certainly there are many other areas of the culture undergoing equally rapid change. Mobile devices like BlackBerries and smartphones are more convenient for reading e-mail and browsing the web than computers, and apps may eventually take the place of the web. The iPad can browse the web and display not only online newspapers and magazines but also movies, e-books, apps of all kinds, social media, and e-mail. Television networks and cable are threatened by the advent of large-screen TVs that can connect directly to the Internet, where movies and shows, music, e-mail, and social networks can be downloaded and accessed. The DVD may be over.

In the music world, easy downloads prevail, and even the CD may someday be a thing of the past. College textbooks are going digital for a fraction of the cost of hardcover copies and will allow professors to add syllabi and make their own changes in the text. Such digital textbooks will eventually train college generations to do their reading online. For that matter, the advent and public acceptance of e-book readers like the Kindle with its lower-priced books threaten hardcover book publishers, who are fighting to make Amazon and other e-book purveyors reprice their digital offerings. Traditional journalism may be on the ropes, but the writing is also on the wall for all these established businesses. Technology has a life of its own and mows down everything in its path.

SCOOPS HAPPEN

One of the first signs of the Internet's incursion on print media was the *Drudge Report,* a political gossip website started by Matt Drudge in the mid-1990s. He was the first to report Bill Clinton's dalliance with Monica Lewinsky, scooping every daily newspaper in the country in 1998 with the revelation and launching a scramble in the national press to cover it. The story of John Edward's $400 haircut during the 2008 election campaign was another Drudge scoop that caught the press unaware.[19] His tabloid-style sensationalism, which he claimed was modeled on that of 1950s gossip columnist Walter Winchell, had brought in one billion plus unique viewers by 2002 and started earning him a million bucks a year by 2008.[20]

Arianna Huffington says the *Drudge Report* was an inspiration for her own launch of the *Huffington Post,* which she claims "could not have existed without Drudge." "I didn't kill newspapers, darling," she said in a speech at the American Association of Advertising Agencies (AAAA) conference in San Francisco in March 2010. "Drudge habituated people to going online for their news."[21] Now she is in the process of hiring her own investigative team of journalists to take over the in-depth reporting and labels *HuffPost* "America's Internet Newspaper."[22]

Professional journalists dread nothing more than being upstaged on breaking news. Even more upsetting is having their stories leak even before they are published. When *Time* magazine contracted with Andre Agassi to publish excerpts from his forthcoming autobiography in *People* and *Sports Illustrated,* a reporter who had read the excerpts posted a tweet—just a day ahead of publication—about Agassi's admission in the book to using crystal meth. The tweet got deleted just 25 minutes later, but it was too late. Public reaction was worldwide. That Sunday, Katie Couric's pretaped interview with Agassi on *60 Minutes* was edited to add this last-minute scoop.

Every public figure who makes inadvertent or ill-advised comments is immediately subject to scrutiny by 24/7 media with a news hole or talk show to fill. Claiming "I was quoted out of context" doesn't stop the endless recycling of such remarks. Dan Rather, who should know better, made a remark about a "watermelon farm" in connection with President Obama that became instant fodder for every media outlet, blogger, and Twitterer in March 2010. Even President Obama made some off-the-cuff remarks during his election campaign about voters in Pennsylvania that, picked up and taped by a freelance journalist, made every news outlet after it was posted on "Off the Bus" on *HuffPost*.[23]

It takes much more time and deliberation to investigate important stories and get the facts in a responsible, journalistic way than it does just to post a headline on the web. Editors at traditional media are there to screen out unverified information and check the facts. A trained, professional journalist investigating a story can uncover far more information than a collection of tweets or a blog can ever offer and can put in the paid time to find it. The *New York Times* holds on to its reputation as the newspaper of record because of its extensive, fact-based coverage of world and local events. Few websites can hire or pay a staff of experienced journalists (and, in fact, most websites still pick up their news stories from newspapers, some word for word, which has led to lawsuits). Now *Forbes* magazine is paying its bloggers by the number of hits their blogs collect. The *Huffington Post,* according to Arianna Huffington, is actively building its own stable of trained investigative reporters, hiring them out of layoff hell as more and more traditional newspaper staff are let go. Freelance journalists freshly "freed" from traditional media abound. But to get rehired, they now often have to be able to handle a camera, shoot the video, do the audio, *and* write the story. As Tina Brown, editor of the online news site the *Daily Beast,* has said, "Nobody I know has a job anymore. They all have gigs."[24]

For comparison of news style and blog style, here are two accounts of a recent brouhaha over a proposal to build a mosque near Ground Zero in New York City. The first, a *New York Times* report, reads:

After a raucous hearing, a Manhattan community board backed a proposal on Tuesday evening to build a Muslim community center near the World Trade Center. The 29-to-1 vote, with 10 abstentions, followed a four-hour back-and-forth between those who said the community center would be a monument to tolerance and those who believed it would be an affront to victims of the 2001 terrorist attacks. The board's vote was advisory—it did not have the power to scrap plans for a center—but it was seen as an important barometer of community sentiment. Middle school students and rabbis were among the more than 100 people who testified at the hearing, which was held a short distance from ground zero. Some carried pictures of family members killed in the attacks; others brandished signs reading "Show respect for 9/11. No mosque!"...The proposed center, called the Cordoba House, would rise as many as 15 stories two blocks north of where the twin towers stood. It would include a prayer space, as well as a 500-seat performing arts center, a culinary school, a swimming pool, a restaurant and other amenities.[25]

A blog reaction, from Kay at *White Noise Insanity:*

> If you've been listening to the big vile mouths of the right wing of this country, you would believe that the Islamic mosque in New York City will be built right on Ground Zero and nowhere else. Those of us with rational brains, however, understand that this mosque will be built *2 blocks from Ground Zero on land that has had a building on it for the last 150 years.* If I'm not mistaken, there once was a Burlington Coat Factory in the building, which to the right wing of this country, a coat factory is a much better way in honoring those Americans who died on the morning of 9/11/01! Right idiots? See? Our country was founded on RELIGIOUS FREEDOMS. How come you right wingers still want to spit in the face of our Founding Fathers? Huh? SIT UP STRAIGHT, WIPE YOUR MOUTHS, AND THEN GROW UP PLEASE! Try to act like adults today, please.[26]

THE J-SCHOOL REVOLUTION

At journalism schools around the country, the curriculum is undergoing rapid revision. Instruction is in multimedia, not just in writing leads and crafting stories. At the Poynter Institute's NewsU, courses now include "Mobile Media 101: Producing News with Your Smartphone," "Building a Twitter Strategy for Your News Organization," and "Newswriting for the Web," along with instruction in visual journalism, photojournalism, graphics, and design. Students learn how to host a podcast and file video stories, design a website, and report across all platforms including online, print, and broadcast. Far different from the usual instruction in "how to write a lead" and the "who, what, when, where, and why" of a news story (though these kinds of skills still have to be taught), this is a totally different lineup of J-school coursework from barely five years ago. It's the new new journalism, turning traditional journalists into one-man bands, maybe even into operating solo as news entrepreneurs, or "backpack journalists" as Dean Charles Bierbauer of the University of South Carolina's College of Mass Communications calls them.[27]

Journalism school professors acknowledge that they don't really know what the future is for news when a web that favors self-expression and instant gratification is the predominant vehicle. Technology may have speeded up the need for news, but a stable political state of informed citizens still requires the kind of in-the-trenches dogged pursuit of fact that has distinguished the best journalism of the past. In the face of speeded-up online eyewitness accounts, looser language, unreliable sourcing, and multiple news outlets, the old rules and standards get bent and forgotten, and unsubstantiated rumors are rife.

HOW I LEARNED TO STOP WORRYING AND LOVE THE WEB

Newspapers and television news stations that want to stay in business are in a mad dash to establish an Internet presence. The *New York Times* is putting up a paywall up around its online site, so far greeted by major outcry from its readers (regular subscribers would get it free). The *Wall Street Journal* has had a paywall in place for its online edition since the beginning and seems not to have suffered a fall in readership. Every network and cable news outlet has a website, so far free for the taking. Getting news readers to pay for these sites, though, would be "like trying to force butterflies back into their cocoons," according to a Pew project study.[28]

In the same study, 15 percent of those surveyed said even with a paywall, they would still visit their favorite news sites (which include Yahoo, MSNBC, AOL, and the *New York Times*). But 82 percent said they would go elsewhere.

That's just the point: Content on the Internet has been and is free for the consumer. Putting up paywalls will in itself cut readership, and advertisers, who buy space on websites according to the numbers of what are called "unique visitors," those who enter the site for the first time and then return, will take note—and take leave. Paywalls are an old-media solution to a new-media problem, and most critics think they won't work. "We can't use an analog map and expect to find our way in a digital world," Arianna Huffington said in her March 2010 keynote speech. The *HuffPost* is free and had been just about breaking even with advertising revenues, she says (now with AOL in charge, stay tuned). Its mix of hard news and soft, with celebrity news, gossip, fashion, and a stable of jazzy, sometimes ideologically tilted bloggers, offers an entirely different image of a newspaper, maybe the one we're headed for.

"It's a tough transition," says Tina Brown, editor of the equally successful (and free) news website the *Daily Beast,* of the current print-into-website situation. But "it will shake out." Some "will flourish, others not."[29] Flourishing, the *Daily Beast* merged with *Newsweek* magazine in November 2010.

If paywalls do take hold, things like embedded links to other sites, and blogs that provide enrichment to a news website, may be lost or locked out under a pay-for-content system. Moreover, the current fights over copyright will get worse, "necessitating a virtual police state to see that there are no unauthorized infringements on the content of the paywall-cartel members," McChesney and Nichols point out, something the waning music industry knows too well and has failed at policing.[30]

THE JOURNALISM OF THE BLOGOSPHERE

As much as any new Internet media, blogs have been instrumental in reshaping the face of journalism and providing more than their fair share of breaking news and op-ed pages. The *Huffington Post* and the *Daily Beast* are essentially blogs or aggregators of blogs, but the online blogosphere itself is huge, comprising some 159,000,000 blogs worldwide.

Blogs, or weblogs as they were first called, started out as fringe elements, guerrilla journalism heavily colored left and right with ideology. Nobody paid much attention to them, and there were certainly reasons not to. Some were written by people with a big axe to grind, while others were nonsensical and trivial. Some still are, but blogs have earned respect as, for the most part, bona fide and intelligent commentary, particularly in the political realm. Major left-wing sites like *Talking Points Memo* and the *Daily Kos* have become must-reads on the left, as have *Outside the Beltway* and *Little Green Footballs* on the right. Respected professional journalists have taken to blogging, like Andrew Sullivan, formerly at *Atlantic. com,* now with *The Daily Beast,* and Scott Rosenberg, cofounder of *Salon.* Everybody who is anybody is in the blogosphere.

There are still no gatekeepers or editors chiseling and correcting the prose, which is part of the appeal for both writers and readers. But major print and television news media have jumped on the blog wagon with whole fleets of staff producing daily blogs, some of them news, many opinion. Most bloggers were sounding off on their own ideas and ideologies, a virtual op-ed of the Internet, and once blogging developed enough (in 2002) to allow readers to post comments, blogs became crucial aggregates of the like-minded, laying the groundwork for the polarized populace that plagues politicians today. There were accusations of bias on the left and bias on the right. Political junkies of every stripe took sides. Anger at then-president Bush fueled plenty of blogs, and so did anger at the mainstream media, keeping stories alive that had been left to die by professional journalists. The war cry out of the blogs to the media: "We can fact-check your ass" (blogger Ken Layne's retort to British journalist whose story he found inaccurate).[31]

It was probably Josh Marshall on *Talking Points Memo,* one of the early blog sites, who earned major points for bloggers by exposing Trent Lott in 2002, reporting day after day on Lott's praise for Strom Thurmond's racially biased run for president during a tribute to Thurmond's 100th birthday. Marshall kept at it. He dug up past similar, segregationist remarks by Lott. This was a story the mainstream media had let lag until it took notice of what Marshall was doing and began to cover it. Two weeks later, Lott announced he was leaving as Senate majority leader. "The Internet's First Scalp" is how John Podhoretz, a conservative columnist for the *New York Post,* titled his column for December 13, 2002.[32]

Howard Dean caught on to the power of blogs early as he conducted his bid for the presidency in 2003, collecting "Deaniacs" and cash and waking the press up to his populist pull. He didn't make it, after screaming in Iowa, but went on to become the Democratic Party chairman.[33]

Barack Obama, though he used the Internet heavily and cleverly during his presidential campaign, essentially ignored the blogosphere, according to Eric Boehlert in *Bloggers on the Bus.*[34] But it didn't matter. Bloggers loved him and wrote about him anyway. Meanwhile, the Obama campaign collected upward of 10 million e-mail addresses and sent a personal message to each of them. People responded with money, volunteered to help get out the vote, and made him president.

The "nowness" of blogs is a challenge to traditional newspapers that have heretofore owned that concept. Organized in reverse chronological order, blogs, to be successful with readers, need up-to-the-minute, right-now freshness. Their premium is what's new, whether it's the latest scoop or the latest commentary. Moreover, blogs create their own community of readers, large or small, enlarging it into interactive comment and related links, something a print newspaper, though it too creates communities of readers, can't offer. The back-and-forth of blog commentary is one of its biggest attractions, as people make an end run around established authority and sound off at will. No wonder the blog is the new public square.

Nontraditional news sources like blogs "can alter the news cycle in profound ways," as the blog *WikiLeaks* did in the summer of 2010 by releasing the Afghan War Diary. This cache of classified documents on how Pakistan was aiding insurgents in Afghanistan set off a firestorm as politicians, government officials, lawyers, and journalists jumped into action and kept the blogosphere going for days. The relentless 24/7 need to fill the news hole, both in print and on television, means that important stories like this—or an emotionally charged issue like a plan to build a mosque and Islamic cultural center near Ground Zero—have a long life, providing plenty of talking points for opinion columns, cable TV shows, and bloggers. There are more pundits than news programs on television, and they need the fuel of debatable issues to keep an increasingly polarized audience watching. Those blog-around-the-clock bloggers keep issues alive, and, as columnist David Carr noted, "the current administration and mainstream media have developed a hair-trigger response after getting run over by stories that seemed to come out of nowhere." The web's speed is "less a tool of efficacy than instigation."[35]

Critics say blogs are fragmenting information and our sense of the world, turning everything into sound bites and quick takes and threatening a more considered understanding of issues and events. Perhaps, but blogs can't take all the blame. They said the same thing about television, by the way, when it first took hold in the 1960s and 1970s. As Scott Rosenberg observes in *Say Everything,* the fear was that "TV would homogenize our communities, brainwash our kids, and rot our brains."[36] Ray Bradbury said that his 1953 book, *Fahrenheit 451,* was intended as a warning "that broadcast television would wreck America by transforming us from a nation of individual readers into an undifferentiated mass of passive viewers."[37] Each new technology is threatening, and the pace of change is at Mach speed these days, engendering similar pronouncements.

Yet it's clear that blogs, which offer free and unlimited self-expression to an interactive readership, are not going away. Major news media, including news networks like CNN, the *New York Times,* the *Wall Street Journal,* and others, are scrambling to establish a presence in the blogosphere, and there are plenty of laid-off professional journalists at the ready to help them. The newest "Brat Pack" of politics in Washington is a group of bloggers, formerly employed elsewhere, now blogging on their own or for *Slate* or other media about insider political news.[38]

THE NEWS AGENDA

A survey of the news agenda of new media versus traditional media that was conducted in 2010 by the Pew Research Center's Project for Excellence in Journalism found that "social media and the mainstream press clearly embrace different agendas. Blogs shared the same lead story with traditional media in just 13 of the 49 weeks studied."[39] Stories gain traction quickly in social media and blogs but leave just as quickly, and the agenda is different, with politics the focus. On Twitter, technology news is a top story, 21 percent, compared to just 1 percent in the mainstream press. Nonetheless, the survey found, blogs still rely on "legacy outlets" such as newspapers and television for 99 percent of their information.

Yahoo introduced a news blog, *The Upshot,* in 2010 that is based on search-generated content. Using software that tracks topics and common words and phrases popular on its network, Yahoo's team analyzes patterns and passes them along to a news staff of bloggers who then write articles targeted to the audience, a boon no doubt to selling ads and a powerful niche approach to its readers. It's "the algorithm as editor," as the *New York Times* puts it, but the idea of writing only news that will sell is anathema to traditional journalism.[40]

The idea is also to give more of an inside angle on the news, something blogs tend to focus on anyway and have proven to be particularly good at. The audience getting news from blogs finds out more of this insider information because blogs aren't muzzled by establishment codes of silence (John Kennedy's escapades in the White House pool would not have been politely overlooked in the age of blogging). Our "culture of exposure," as David Brooks says, is about "inside baseball," finding out "the inner soap opera" behind the news, as General McChrystal learned to the dismay of the president. The kvetching that goes on behind the scenes is now headline news.[41]

Perhaps because blogs and Twitter are highly individualized communiqués, intended for a narrower audience, their stories are customized and take different angles on the news compared to mainstream media. Indeed, they tend to be far less bland in style than traditional news stories, which have to reach a much broader readership. Moreover, without editors and gatekeepers to put a lid on self-expression, online media have much more room for opinion and political agendas. Blogs are often written in the first person, underscoring a subjective, personal take. And they are embedded with links, giving them a much wider reach than traditional news stories. Blogs and Twitter are also aiming for reader response, so they are often confrontational, bringing up the most controversial issues. Formerly voices of the counterculture, blogs and Twitter *are* the culture now, "picking off mainstream media's customers one by one," as Chris Anderson notes in his book, *The Long Tail.*[42]

One of the real and present dangers of Internet information is how readily it can become misinformation. There are plenty of blogs and websites out there happy to spread or start rumors that quickly go viral, to say nothing of Nigerian scams, foreign lotteries, work-at-home offers, urban legends, and cybersmears. Scientists complain about the way the web spreads rumors about scientific discoveries at the speed of light, possibly the result of preliminary experiments that eager researchers want to announce, for example, a rumor about a discovery of the subatomic particles of dark matter that proved to be inaccurate.[43] News itself is prone to misinformation and lack of coverage, with Twitter reports streaming in with breaking news from disaster areas. The Internet is also a place where propaganda has more than a half-life, as North Korea has discovered, smearing South Korea on Twitter and YouTube and calling Secretary of State Hillary Rodham Clinton "a minister in a skirt" and Secretary of Defense Robert Gates a "war maniac."[44] Farhad Manjoo, author of *True Enough: Learning to Live in a Post-Fact Society,* observes, "When we strung up the planet in fiber-optic cable, when we dissolved the mainstream media into prickly niches, and when each of us began to create and transmit our own pictures and sounds, we eased the path through which propaganda infects the culture."[45]

CITIZEN JOURNALISM

A report by a volunteer journalist, Mayhill Fowler, on remarks Barack Obama made at a fund-raiser she attended virtually changed the course of his campaign. She was there as a donor to his 2008 election campaign but routinely taped what Obama had to say. Eventually, her report was published in "Off the Bus" on the *Huffington Post* website. She reported (and taped) that Obama had, to all intents and purposes, dissed the small-town voters of Pennsylvania by characterizing them as "bitter, clinging to guns or religion or antipathy to people who aren't like them or anti-immigrant sentiment or anti-trade sentiment as a way to explain their frustrations."[46] The comments became known as Bittergate and spawned "55 digital pages" of hate mail to Fowler and the *HuffPost*. Obama, who had taken full advantage of the Internet and social media networks to conduct his election campaign, got his first taste of the negatives in going viral.

Fowler was not a professional journalist, but she carried a tape recorder, and she'd already had another major scoop, reporting on something Bill Clinton casually said on a rope line in South Dakota during the campaign. She had asked him about the recent *Vanity Fair* article deriding Clinton's activities since he left office. Not realizing that he was being taped or that Fowler was a citizen journalist, Clinton let rip with a three-minute diatribe about the "dishonest reporter" who wrote the magazine article. Fowler transcribed the taped remarks to her BlackBerry and sent them to her editor at "Off the Bus" at the *Huffington Post*. Within hours, it was a *HuffPost* headline: "Bill Clinton: Purdum a 'Sleazy' 'Slimy' 'Scumbag,'" and producers for Anderson Cooper and Keith Olbermann were asking for the audio.[47]

Such are the triumphs and perils of citizen journalism in the age of the Internet. Print journalists know they have to keep up with online news blogs and social media to be able to write their own stories and pick up news tips. The BBC even sent out a directive to its news staff in February 2010 requiring them to use social media as a primary source. "It's not discretionary," Peter Horrocks, director of BBC Global Media, told them, noting that "technology is changing journalism" and the BBC has to leave a program-based mindset behind and adapt.[48]

ARE BLOGS AND TWITTER HIJACKING JOURNALISM?

Yes, in some significant ways, Twitter and blogs are hijacking journalism, with breaking news and fast-moving, up-to-the-minute content, with a more intimate, subjective (and opinionated) take on the news, and with the interactivity that draws in an active, interested audience.

No, because blogs and Twitter can't match the kind of in-depth coverage the major mainstream press, with its teams of professional investigative reporters and international news bureaus, can offer. This is going to change, however, as online blog sites like *Huffington Post* and the *Daily Beast* beef up their reportorial staffs and become full-fledged online newspapers in their new alliances, *HuffPost* with AOL and The *Daily Beast* with *Newsweek*.

SIX

Language in a Twittering, Blogging World

On the web, the word is ascendant. People have to read and they have to write in order to participate in social media, e-mail, texting, instant messaging, blogs, and Twitter. Not to say they haven't found shortcut ways of communicating and given the language some new twists. What they are writing and reading is more like conversation, unedited, expressive, and, sometimes, blue. We're back in an oral culture, as Marshall McLuhan predicted, sorting ourselves out into tribes on the Internet and talking to each other more than ever. Hey, it's free. Sometimes it's a free-for-all.

Even though visual information gets to the brain faster and is rapidly becoming the communication vehicle of choice (e.g., YouTube), print culture continues in a new, viral form online. It has been translated into emoticons like smiley faces, abbreviations, plenty of acronyms (LOL), and considerable slang and new coinage, but (OMG) you still have to read to be online. There are brand-new verbs: to "friend," "google," "text," "tweet," "download," to say nothing of a profusion of new nouns and proper nouns like blog, Wikipedia, YouTube, Facebook, and Twitter. Even the revered *Oxford English Dictionary* decided to add the initialisms LOL, OMG, and FYI to its venerable pages in 2011, to the consternation of language mavens.

Without editors or gatekeepers, language on the Internet is in constant flux, experimental at best, ungrammatical at worst. Online, language has more immediacy and the flavor of conversation. It is in casual, informal dress, like much of culture, and thus not always presentable. Yet experts who study these things say that language offline has not been measurably affected, that students can still put together coherent papers in full sentences, and, even, that all the extra writing they are doing online is improving their mastery of written language. The Internet is not to blame for a decades-long trend toward a more informal, speech-based style, what linguistics professor Naomi S. Baron, author of *Always On,* calls "linguistic whateverism," a new laissez-faire attitude in which the rules of language matter less than getting the message across. She suggests that the English language may revert to the "quasi-anarchy of medieval and even Renaissance England," where even "William Shakespeare spelled his own name at least six different ways."[1] Under the influence of the Internet, language will, as is its wont, continue to evolve.

Hamlet's famous soliloquy would look like this in texting or on Twitter: 2b/or/not2b.

CYBERSTYLE

Out in the culture, language is getting bolder as standards erode in public speech and on television. Perhaps it's inevitable to pick up the common parlance of the streets. Even though a "family newspaper" can't print some of it, advertisers online, on TV, or in print are resorting to more earthy talk to push their wares, sometimes bleeping themselves (with plenty of innuendo to make sure consumers get it) or using strategic dashes. The idea of all the frank street talk is to show they mean business and, maybe, stir up some attention-getting controversy. But an editor of the *Guardian's Observer,* Stephen Pritchard, noting that 272 recent *Guardian* articles included the f-word, argues that though he finds it distasteful, "It is sometimes necessary to report verbatim what somebody says if you are to give a truly accurate picture of their character."[2]

Vulgarity is increasingly tolerated, on the web, in print, even on broadcast television, though the brokerage firm Goldman Sachs had to issue a directive banning profanity in its e-mails. However, even President Obama, in an interview with Matt Lauer on the *Today* show, resorted to an unusual "kicking-ass" comment, perhaps to emphasize an emotional effect he is often accused of lacking. We do "accidentally let things slip," especially online, as Aaron Barlow comments in *Blogging America.*[3] And you can't edit your text messages, tweets, or e-mails after you send them, which makes room for the same gaffes you might make in real conversation.

Blogs seem to bring out bold language, and male bloggers feel free to use it, spicing up their posts with intentionally provocative comments and humor. One typical kind of sentence: "Where does the rise of the app leave the news business, the flatulent Rottweiler in the dog shelter of online content?" asked Adrian Monck in his blog for the *Guardian*.[4]

Another sample comes from *Gawker* blogger Adrian Chen, writing about North Korea's new Facebook, Twitter, and YouTube accounts:

> So ... North Korea—owner of the world's fourth-largest army, population 23 million—has just 65 friends, is gay, and interested in networking? And most of the activity on North Korea's wall has been by a guy named "Jonathan Raptor Kraus." Frankly, this looks more like the profile page of a middle-aged manager of a Secaucus, NJ Hollister than a nuclearized Communist state. And why would they open a personal page instead of a fan page? Some prankster is going to tag North Korea in a Facebook Places check at the White House and World War III will start![5]

Gawker is a popular gossip blog, known for its snarky style. In fact, there are even rules about "How to Write Like *Gawker*," including these compiled by Dylan Stableford in *Folio:*

- Put back "the Gawkeresque angry-creative-underclass glint" in your voice, "one glint of nastiness per post."
- "If someone screwed up in business, find something nice to say about them: 'The charmingly incompetent CEO.' If someone succeeded, find a way to slap them: 'The wildly successful blowhard.'"
- Be edgy and insulting: "Voting for Ron Paul sends a message. The message is you're crazy and hate the FDA."
- "If you wouldn't say it in conversation, don't write it. Avoid journalist-speak like 'He takes umbrage with our statement.' You never say umbrage in real life."
- Use satire and parody: "President Steve Jobs issues the most expensive U.S. budget ever, but it fits in a manila envelope."[6]

In contrast, women bloggers, though they do try for humor and snarkiness, tend to be more empathetic and adhere to standard usage. Here is Heather Armstrong writing about her baby daughter on *Dooce.com,* a favorite mommy blog:

> Marlo's favorite thing to do now, after having been taught by her evil grandmother, is to climb stairs. Great. Because this new house

is basically four stories, three above and one below ground. Lots of stairs to climb! No problem for an almost thirteen-month-old who routinely dives off of our bed head-first and loves the sound her skull makes as it hits the floor!

For the first few days we were living here we didn't have the right size of gate to install in areas where a gate might help things out. So while unpacking we would take turns grabbing her from the bottom of the staircase, returning her to a safe spot, and then grabbing her again. Over and over and over, and I finally understood why some women say they stay thin because they chase after their children. Because before, *there was no chasing.* It was me in one corner folding clothes while Leta [older daughter] sat perfectly still on the couch reading Chaucer.[7]

Armstrong has her own brand of edge (her website name, "dooced," she says, stands for being fired for blogging): "Who in their right mind would buy a house like this, right? Let's just put it this way: have you seen my bathtub? Fifteen minutes in that thing is like four shots of bourbon, and suddenly everything is fine and next thing you know you're drunk-dialing friends and slurring *YOU ARE SO NICE, I LIKE YOU.*"[8]

The editor of the *Hollywood Reporter* website, Janice Min, attracted attention in late August 2010 for putting this headline on a movie review, "'Switch'a Bitch for Jennifer Aniston," possibly the first use of the b-word in a newspaper and setting a new tone for the publication. Journalists claimed to be shocked.[9]

The new *Yahoo! Style Guide,* issued in the spring of 2010 and calling itself "The Ultimate Sourcebook for Writing, Editing, and Creating Content for the Digital World," tries to codify online writing style, with tips in the first chapter for streamlining your style for cyberspace:

1. Shape text for online reading: That is, keep sentences short to allow scanning.

2. Get to the point fast, keep it short, and use common, short words: "Your content has a few seconds—three or less!—to encourage people to read more."

3. Use good headlines, subheads, and bulleted points to allow scanning.

4. Write to appeal to the widest possible audience: People reading your words may be younger or older, less knowledgeable or proficient, or less adept at English. They might be in Antarctica or Zambia.

5. Write clear links and provide some context for them.[10]

The Yahoo! guide also offers advice on identifying an audience and gauging the readability of writing, as well as basics of grammar, punctuation, capitalization, and other rules.

Many of these rules for writing are already well known to journalists who are used to front-loading their stories, writing short sentences for easier reading and narrow print newspaper columns, and using that bible of style, the *Associated Press Stylebook.* Yet online writing, particularly in blogs, has acquired a feeling of freshness and immediacy different from the standard (and vetted) style of print journalism. It has a conversational tone, and because most blogs are written in the first person—not allowed in the objective world of a news report—writing takes on an intimacy and directness that does feel like talking face to face. Cyberstyle is more user-friendly, not the rhetoric of the establishment but of the everyday, ordinary world.

MASHUP: WORDS

What computers and the Internet tend to do is magnify these trends, Naomi Baron says.[11] We *are* doing more writing, of necessity online. Many adults, used to not writing anything at all, are now writing on the Internet. Yet, as McLuhan predicted, we're becoming an oral culture, and our use of language on the Internet reflects that. Looser, casual, not-always-grammatical language, like conversation, is the coin of the realm in blogs and e-mail, on Twitter and social media, and, certainly, in texting. This language sounds much more like spoken than written language, even on-screen. Though a writer may be well aware of correct spelling and usage, it's faster and easier to say "U" or "b/c," skip the capitalization, and write in short sound bites rather than complete sentences (when the telegraph first came on the scene in the 19th century, similar shortcuts emerged, as people were charged by the word).

New words are naturally coined daily in the language, but the Internet has them coming at Mach 2 speed. Mashups (a new word from the web, meaning a remix or blend of digital material to create something new) abound: *blog* of course, a blend of *web* and *log; webinar* for a seminar online; *emoticon* (*emote* plus *icon*); Facebook. Then there are words we're getting used to like *browser,* a noun made out of a verb; *avatar,* now the title of a major motion picture; *icon*; *phishing* (hoax e-mail).

Slang is always the most volatile area of language, and it generates the freshest new words (or, as scholars say, neologisms). Primarily, the role of slang is to separate the "in" group from the "out," fencing off the cool kids from the clueless, like parents. The amount of slang being generated now by the web is huge, and it travels faster than ever on the web, accessible from one continent to the next at the speed of light when it might have taken 20 years before the Internet. Slang words have a shorter shelf life than they used to, but there are still 2,500 slang words for "drunk," and some websites, like *Gawker,* are trying to curb some ubiquitous slang phrases on blogs and Twitter like "I'm just saying," often used to defang a confrontational comment.[12]

Old words are enjoying new status: For example, the word *so* is now used at the beginning of sentences, linguists note, rather than as a connective in the middle. *So* carries a hint of logic, like *thus* and *therefore, so-*ing things together in an increasingly fragmented world of online discourse. Microsoft employees claim that the *so* boom began with them, an "if this, then that" connective that appealed to engineers. It's also a way of staying on message in a tweeting, posting, blogging world where the certitude of black-and-white statement has a way of crowding out the gray.[13]

GENDER BENDER

There's evidence that women use language differently than men do on the web, but according to Baron, we still don't know enough about these online differences because most gender studies have dealt with spoken, not written language. Deborah Tannen's work on language has shown that, in general, women prefer face-to-face conversation and eye contact, both of which are missing on the Internet. Tannen's book, *You Just Don't Understand: Men and Women in Conversation,* is still an authoritative text on the subject.[14]

Baron says that women also tend to use more qualifiers, are more polite, stick to standard usage, and use conversation to enhance social interaction, while men converse to convey information.[15] Susan Herring, editor of the collection *Computer-Mediated Communication: Linguistic, Social, and Cross-Cultural Perspectives,*[16] found that women online still used many qualifiers, expressed support of others, and displayed many of the social and involved characteristics of female speech patterns, with "three times as many representations of smiles or laughter" as men used.[17] Herring offers these examples of gender differences:

Figure 1. A male posting to a discussion group (responding to a male message)
>yes, they did ... This is why we must be allowed to remain armed ... >who is going to help us if our government becomes a tyranny? >no one will.

oh yes we *must* remain armed. anyone see day one last night abt charlestown where everyone/s so scared of informing on murderers the cops have given up ? where the reply to any offense is a public killing ? knowing you/re not gonna be caught cause everyone/s to afraid to be a witness ? yeah, right, twerp.
>——[Ron] "the Wise"——
what a joke.

Figure 2. A female posting to a discussion group (responding to a female message)
>Aileen, > >I just wanted to let you know that I have really enjoyed all your >posts about Women's herstory. They have been extremely >informative and I've learned alot about the women's movement. >Thank you! > >-Erika
DITTO!!!! They are wonderful!
Did anyone else catch the first part of a Century of Women? I really enjoyed it. Of course, I didn't agree with everything they said. ... but it was really informative.
Roberta~~~~~~~~~~~~~~~~~~~~~~~~~~~~~~~[18]

Though men tend to be more adversarial and dominate the conversation online, there is some sense of gender equality, perhaps because it's difficult to read gender from the words of a tweet or blog. And it's hard to detect deceit. Women can disguise themselves and impersonate a man unless they break out of stereotypes and are discovered. Female aggression or threatening behavior can arouse criticism, because an audience who discovers her gender may feel she shouldn't be acting that way, Patricia Wallace, author of *The Psychology of the Internet,* says.[19] Online, people do tend to rely on categories and stereotypes because the nonverbal cues, the body language and facial expressions, are missing. Webcams and Skype change that scenario, however.

WICKED FAST

Speed and immediacy are part of the attraction of texting and tweeting, which are much faster than e-mail, but the lure is that writing these is also like a game. On a cell phone or on Twitter, it's a challenge to fit the message into the constraint of 140 characters. Hence the abbreviations and acronyms, which are not all new. Remember RSVP and BYOB, FYI, and now TMI (too much information)? Even the @ in e-mail addresses is short for "located at." And even the YMCA is downsizing its acronym to just Y, the nickname already in use. Sound bites are big, sometimes substituting for even bigger ideas and becoming memes on the Internet, as in the 2008 presidential campaign: "You can put lipstick on a pig" was recycled 690 times in the three months leading up to the election, according to a Cornell University study.[20]

One would think that texting, which is driving people off the road and keeping teenagers busy at a rate of 100 texts a day, would, with its cryptic characters, really be ruining the language. Not at all, according to professional linguist David Crystal, author of *Txting: The Gr8 Db8*. Despite the more than a trillion text messages sent every year worldwide, Crystal says they "appear as no more than a few ripples on the surface of the sea of language." "People were playing with language in this way long before mobile phones were invented."[21] As Louis Menand points out in a *New Yorker* article about Crystal's book, texting (and tweeting) may actually favor English, which has shorter words (on average, five letters) than other languages, and it's cool to use English in other countries.[22]

Another attraction of texting, according to Menand, is that "people dread face-to-face exchanges" that require "a real, unscripted conversation": "People don't like to have to perform the amount of self-presentation that is required in a personal encounter. They don't want to deal with the facial expressions, the body language, the obligation to be witty or interesting. They just want to say 'flt is lte.'[flight is late]."[23]

Writers learn to "emote" in words, as Clay Shirky, professor of new media at New York University, observes. Online, there is "a huge premium on verbal acuity while conveying none of the emotional cues you pick up from other people when you are in the same physical space with them."[24]

THE GRAMMAR POLICE

But the state of online language has generated an unofficial Twitter patrol, a kind of subculture of grammar vigilantes who let other Twitterati know when they've committed spelling and grammar errors. Just keeping up the Twetiquette, don't you know. Needless to say, there's a lot of backlash. Pet targets of these language watchdogs are those who write their tweets in all caps or use the wrong words or incorrect verb forms. They also alert tweeters to just plain stupidity. The watchdogs claim that the response they get—mostly angry rant—is worth it. Several Twitter accounts, like "Twenglish Police," "You or Youre," "Grammar Fail," and "Grammar Hero." patrol the site.[25] On the air there are gaffes in written scripts. The CEO of the Tribune Co. in Chicago, Randy Michaels, got so incensed over clichés that anchors and reporters on WGN-AM used that he issued a list of 119 forbidden words and phrases, including "at this point in time," "close proximity," "bare naked," "no brainer," and "went terribly wrong." "The real goal here," he said, "is to avoid using words that make you sound like you're reading, instead of talking—that shatter the image you're speaking knowledgeably to one person. By not using 'newsspeak,' you enhance your reputation as a communicator."[26]

One blog, *Language Log,* keeps track of all these new quirks in the language in a witty way, especially when it comes to the grammar police, whom it finds off base in their fervor to save the world from linguistic decline. The blog features "Crash Blossoms," ambiguous headlines in the news; "Eggcorns," malapropisms people coin when they mishear and mispronounce words (like "cut to the cheese" instead of "cut to the chase"); and "Nerdviews," which can be found in the directions of any appliance instruction manual you own, including computers. The group blog, produced at the University of Pennsylvania, has resulted in a book culled from blog posts, *Far from the Madding Gerund.*[27]

READWRITEWEB

Academic writing instructors also say the more casual language of the Internet has had less effect than one would think on formal writing. Professor Andrea Lunsford, director of Stanford University's Writing and Rhetoric Program, says that students are writing more because of the Internet, more than any previous generation in history. And they are writing in an exciting new context, online, where the audience and the writer merge, an incalculably helpful situation for any writer. In her five-year "Stanford Study of Writing, 2001–2005," Lunsford invited a random sample of students in the Stanford freshman class to submit all their writing, both personal and from classwork, during their four years at the university and in the year after graduating. She says she found their writing was rich and complex, adept at adjusting to different audiences, and very aware of its power to effect change.[28]

Especially interesting, Lunsford says, is the kind of "epistemic" or exploratory writing the students did in blogs and on social media, where you write before you are sure of what you are going to say and where creative, interesting ideas often emerge. This is writing "about instantaneous communication." But "college writers need to be able to retain the best of print literacy, and know how to deploy it for their own purposes," Lunsford says. And "they also need and deserve to be exposed to new forms of expression," which their online lives are giving them, opening up their perspective on other ways of writing around the world. For those who are wondering "whether Google is making us stupid and whether Facebook is frying our brains," Lunsford says, this study refutes that conventional view and shows that student writing is very much alive and well in the new context of the Internet.[29]

Though the Stanford study shows the unique evolution of online writing, the quality of student writing had been deteriorating for years before the Internet came on the scene. Part of the problem is that students are not doing the amount of reading they need to become familiar with how written language is supposed to look. Reading scores in American schools are nothing to brag about and have not been showing improvement. They are, in fact, "stagnant," as the *New York Times* reported in the spring of 2010. "The [reading] scores continue a 17-year trend of sluggish achievement in reading," the *Times* noted, citing educators' opinions that "surfing the Internet, texting on cell phones, or watching television" has made inroads on students' reading abilities, taking priority over reading for pleasure. Based on national tests, from the 1990s to 2009, average reading scores for fourth and eighth graders have risen only four points, "less than half a school year's worth of reading." Math scores, in contrast, have risen 20 points for eighth graders and 27 points for fourth graders.[30]

Reading assignments and instruction in school tend to decline after the early grades, some say, and this is also blamed for the falloff in reading skills. But adults are no longer reading at the same rate they used to (a familiar comment is "But I read the review"), if figures for adult book sales (except for e-books) tell the tale. These were down 1.8 percent in 2009 compared to the usual 1.1 percent average yearly increase. Young adult books dropped even lower, down 5 percent.[31] If newspaper and magazine circulation is down, it's partly because people don't have time to read them, particularly those of the younger generation, who prefer to get information in shorter takes online or on television. Entertainment is more important than news to this group. One study showed that 8- to 18-year-olds are spending, on average, more than seven-and-a-half hours a day online with social media and games or on cell phones and watching television.[32]

Less grammar and writing instruction in grade school and high school—does anyone still diagram sentences?—and a general dislike and even fear of writing persist, even among business executives, who often hire others to do their written work. It takes time to learn to write and to teach it (some say it cannot really be taught). And it takes thought, which may be where the Internet has intervened. Used to multitasking and sped-up responses, writers may shortcut more than their words. Certainly writing e-mail and comments on social media or 140-word statements on Twitter does not lend itself to intricate argument or deep thought.

But writing itself is a way to think and organize one's ideas. Writing is difficult precisely because it requires extended threads of thought and connection. It requires drafts and editing and proofreading to produce something worth a reader's focused time. Self-expression is one thing; a sustained argument is something else again. There are writers who still produce their works in longhand, who find the act of connecting hand and pen to paper helps them think. Writing on computer is faster and facilitates revision, but because it's easier, it may be sloppier.

Still, what we're getting in blogs and on Twitter is much fresher and often more candid in tone than content from more established print media, where the attempt to reach a broad audience can tamp down expressiveness and seem bland compared to bloggers who are mouthing off. One of the reasons professional journalists make it a point to check blogs and Twitter is that the information is unfiltered and, sometimes, truer than the official and edited versions. However, there aren't any editors to catch errors or check facts on Twitter or blogs, and rumors and half-truths may go undetected.

OUR NETBRAINS

In our personal lives, we still write, take notes, and jot down "to do" lists and keep journals, but now much of this is done online, on a cell phone, BlackBerry, or iPad. The act of writing (or typing) something down gives the brain something to look at and build on. But Nicholas Carr, whose recent book, *The Shallows,* explores the way being online affects the brain, is worried about what's happening. Carr also wrote a controversial article in the *Atlantic* in 2008, "Is Google Making Us Stupid? What the Internet Is Doing to Our Brains"; in it, he comments,

> Over the past few years I've had an uncomfortable sense that someone, or something, has been tinkering with my brain, remapping the neural circuitry, reprogramming the memory. My mind isn't going—so far as I can tell—but it's changing. I'm not thinking the way I used to think. I can feel it most strongly when I'm reading. Immersing myself in a book or a lengthy article used to be easy. My mind would get caught up in the narrative or the turns of the argument, and I'd spend hours strolling through long stretches of prose. That's rarely the case anymore. Now my concentration often starts to drift after two or three

By permission of Steve Breen and Creators Syndicate, Inc.

pages. I get fidgety, lose the thread, begin looking for something else to do. I feel as if I'm always dragging my wayward brain back to the text. The deep reading that used to come naturally has become a struggle.[33]

Carr says that a five-year neurological and psychological study underway by scholars at University College London has so far shown a definite trend among Internet users toward "skimming" and "power browsing" material. "Experiments demonstrate that readers of ideograms, such as the Chinese, develop a mental circuitry for reading that is very different from the circuitry found in those of us whose written language employs an alphabet," Carr says,[34] citing the work of Maryanne Wolf, a developmental psychologist at Tufts University and author of *Proust and the Squid: The Story and Science of the Reading Brain.* The Internet may be training the circuits of our brains in new ways, as Wolf says, toward "decoding" rather than interpreting.[35]

Moreover, the ubiquity of the Internet, Carr says, "is subsuming most of our other intellectual technologies. It's becoming our map and our clock, our printing press and our typewriter, our calculator and our telephone, and our radio and TV."[36] However, in *Everything Bad Is Good for You,* Steven Johnson argues that the increasing complexity and range of media we engage with have, over the past century, made us smarter rather than dumber, by providing a form of cognitive calisthenics.[37] And in an article replying to Carr's a year later in the *Atlantic,* "Get Smarter," Jamais Cascio argued that we are developing a different kind of cognition:

> Scientists describe these skills as our "fluid intelligence"—the ability to find meaning in confusion and to solve new problems, independent of acquired knowledge. Fluid intelligence doesn't look much like the capacity to memorize and recite facts, the skills that people have traditionally associated with brainpower. But building it up may improve the capacity to think deeply that Carr and others fear we're losing for good. And we shouldn't let the stresses associated with a transition to a new era blind us to that era's astonishing potential. We swim in an ocean of data, accessible from nearly anywhere, generated by billions of devices. We're only beginning to explore what we can do with this knowledge-at-a-touch.[38]

IS THE BOOK DYING?

Texts are becoming unstable in the online environment. As e-books, they can be revised, annotated, animated with video, and more. These are now being called "enhanced" or "enriched" digital books by traditional publishers, who are freaking out as the e-reader and the e-book increasingly threaten their reason for being—the physical, dead-tree, acid-paper-printed book. Amazon, the giant online bookseller, made history in July 2010 when it announced that sales of e-books for its e-reader, the Kindle, had surpassed sales of hardcover books, with a total of 143 e-books for every 100 hardcover books purchased. A measure of the speed at which this is happening: Amazon had been selling hardcover books for 15 years and e-books for just 33 months.[39]

The writing is on the wall (make that the screen) for the book-publishing industry: Digital books never wear out (or go out of print), and they don't take up shelf space. Customers can download the books they want at bargain prices and carry them around by the dozens. On an e-reader, they can adjust the type size. And, a bonus for romance fans and others, nobody can see the cover of the book you're reading.

Moreover, Google Books (http://www.googlebooks.com) is at work scanning every book in every library on earth at a rate of 1,000 pages an hour, including books in the public domain, books under copyright, and out-of-print books, saying it plans to complete the project in under 10 years. The arrival of e-readers like the Kindle, Nook, and iPad and the lower prices of e-books are luring people to digital reading. E-textbooks with video, as well as custom chapters and syllabi, are training a whole generation of students to read and study online. Libraries themselves are moving into digital books that patrons can "borrow" and download at home (after the allotted borrowing time, the book will disappear from the digital device or computer).

In Japan, whole novels are being written right on cell phones, some of them going on to become best sellers. Mostly these are love stories written by young women. One, a 22-year-old named Rin, wrote a novel while commuting to high school. Published on a website, it was picked up by a publisher, turned into a hardcover book, and sold 400,000 copies, ranking seventh on Japanese best-seller lists in 2007.[40]

Indeed, anyone can now publish his or her own book, online or in print. Blogs have proven to provide rich fodder for a book, whether self-published or "discovered" by a traditional publisher. The book spawned by the *I Can Has Cheezburger?* website is now in its fifth printing, and dozens of other books (and movies) have arisen from blogs, including, most notably, *Julie and Julia,* which the author blogged during a year of cooking every recipe in Julia Child's cookbook and which became a movie. Your self-published print book can be sold on Amazon, where it might catch the eye of an established publisher, and Apple recently announced that you can sell your book in its iBookstore, in several countries.[41]

Twitter offers its own challenges to writers, some of whom have already tried composing on it, including author Rick Moody, who put together a 153-tweet short story. While it's gotten much harder to get a book published by a traditional publishing house these days, would-be authors can easily publish and pay for their own editions in print or online. There are reputable self- publishing companies that can assist with the details and production of your own book (though the marketing and book tour are up to you).

The book isn't dying, but its metamorphosis into digital language is changing our relationship with the world of literature and our culture. We probably won't ever be living in a totally postprint world, but the book as e-book is becoming more visual, with embedded video, maps, illustrations, and links—and now advertising—to expand the understanding of the text. For example, a new edition of one book published in 2008,

Nixonland, now has 27 videos, including interviews, news clips, and the Nixon–Kennedy debates. Some are predicting that e-book publishers will be offering single chapters of books for 99 cents. Books will become more social, according to Clive Thompson: "You'll be able to cut, paste, and exchange your favorite passages, using them in the same promiscuous way we now use online text and video to argue, think, or express how we're feeling."[42] Uninterrupted pages of text really can't compare—or compete. Digital visionary Nicholas Negroponte says, "The paper book is dead."[43]

Clay Shirky of New York University says he thinks "long-form expressive fiction will suffer (though this suffering has been more or less constant since the invention of radio) while all numeric and graphic forms of rendering knowledge, from the creation and use of databases to all forms of visual display of data will be in a golden age, with ordinary non-fiction writing getting a modest boost. So, English majors lose, engineering wins, and what looks like an Up or Down question says more about the demographic of the answerer than any prediction of the future."[44]

"In preparation for landing, please turn off your books."

© Ward Sutton/The New Yorker Collection/www.cartoonbank.com

PLAGIARISM

Anyone who has taught a high school or college course, online or in the classroom, can testify that one of the biggest writing problems now is plagiarism. Not only does the Internet make such "borrowing" tempting and easy, but sometimes students don't even understand that they've plagiarized or what plagiarism is. With so much information at their fingertips, written and ready to go, they seem to feel it's all there for the taking, and they see nothing wrong with taking it. Even prominent authors such as historian Stephen Ambrose, author of *The Wild Blue* about World War II bomber crews, and Doris Kearns Goodwin, author of *The Fitzgeralds and the Kennedys,* as well as several other well-known authors, have been accused of plagiarism. These authors tend to blame it on "my notes."

Plagiarism, essentially, is presenting as your own the words of someone else, without attribution. Vice President Joe Biden once was caught using the unattributed words of British Labor Party leader Neil Kinnock in a stump speech for his own campaign for the presidency in 1988. Biden dropped out of the race in the uproar when the press uncovered more examples of words he had used from Robert Kennedy and Hubert Humphrey.

Two teenage authors who wrote best sellers recently were discovered to have lifted large portions of their novels from other novels. A novel about club life published in 2010 by Berlin author Helene Hegeman, 17, was at the number-five spot on best-seller lists and won a $20,000 prize at the Leipzig Book Fair before it was disclosed that her book, *Axolotl Roadkill,* was heavily laced with passages from another novel. "There's no such thing as originality anyway, just authenticity," the young author said, claiming it was just a "mixing."[45] Another teenager, Harvard freshman Kaavya Viswanathan, had sold her first novel, *How Opal Mehta Got Kissed, Got Wild, and Got a Life,* to Little, Brown in a two-book deal for six figures in 2006. But after it became clear how much of the novel was plagiarized, it was removed from the market and taken out of print.[46]

The Internet may be "redefining how students—who came of age with music file-sharing, Wikipedia and Web-linking—understand the concept of authorship and the singularity of any text or image."[47] Information "just seems to be hanging out there in cyberspace and doesn't have an author," Teresa Fishman, director of the Center for Academic Integrity at Clemson University, says, so students think it's just there "for anyone to take."[48]

Anthropologist Susan D. Blum at the University of Notre Dame told the *New York Times* she thinks the way that social networking allows students to try on "many different personas" may blur their concept of unique identity. In other words, the whole idea of a mashup of identity might make it no big deal to use other people's words and ideas.[49]

LANGUAGE IN A POSTPRINT WORLD

There's no question that the Internet is going to change the English language and already has. We are in fact using our language in new ways, inventing new words, talking and writing to each other in different modes because of the online lives we now live. The bigger question, one that has been under investigation for years, is whether the language we speak and write affects the way we think.

It is a perennial question, one to which there are still no definitive answers but about which there is much speculation. Certainly the environment, both physical and intellectual, affects the way a culture's vocabulary encodes differences. For example, there is a popular belief that Eskimo society needs something like 26 words for snow (the English language has maybe 12). The idea has been discredited as just a legend: The Eskimo language, which works on compounds and adds suffixes, has in reality just a few basic root words that can be finely honed to distinguish one set of snow circumstances from another. Yet that flexible vocabulary is certainly useful when you are surrounded by the white stuff.

Concepts of color and direction have been studied to greater effect. The Russian language allows for far more visual discrimination of shades of blue, for example. In Spanish and Japanese, causality is dropped, so a speaker would be likely to say, "The vase broke itself," rather than "John broke the vase." The missing link, however, is why these languages allow these perceptions, yet linguists agree that the structure of the language we speak does shape the way we think. "The next steps are to understand the mechanisms through which languages help us construct the incredibly complex knowledge systems we have," Lera Boroditsky, professor of psychology at Stanford University, says. "Understanding how knowledge is built will allow us to create ideas that go beyond the currently thinkable."[50]

The language of computer programming is put together by humans for machines—computers—to use. Highly abstract and artificial, such "language" deliberately takes out ambiguities and is streamlined for efficiency and precision (some say rigidity), the things human language, with its constantly evolving meaning, does not control. Both are used for communication, but the semantics and syntax of a computer programming language are defined and codified. Yet computer programming language, which relies on detecting patterns, does not readily understand a metaphor, that construction that compares one thing to another ("my love is a rose").

The language human beings use, for all its ambiguity and volatility, is still the best instrument for understanding the world. How will it evolve under the pressure of the Internet age? A quasi-anarchy may prevail as it did in Shakespeare's England, but now as then, when the culture is in flux, sprouting new words and ideas, great bursts of creativity may unfold. The English language can handle it.

SEVEN

Issues in the Age of Oversharing

The intense interactivity and self-disclosure that the web invites have opened the door to some major issues of privacy, copyright, surveillance, and government monitoring (or blocking) of data. French philosopher Michel Foucault predicted in the 1970s that the advance of technology would lead to accelerated surveillance of the populace. Today, there are more surveillance devices than he ever dreamed of, including the Internet and social media, cell phones, ATMs, credit cards, the census, and the increasing number of surveillance cameras everywhere. Because data on the Internet never go away, it's easy for outside parties to measure our online activities and proclivities. We may not realize we are being watched—and tracked—all the time. Our posts on social media and our purchases and clicks on online advertising create a rich record—how about that Amazon wish list you keeping adding to—of our consumer preferences for advertisers and businesses who are hungry to retrieve and use it to find out more about us.

Indeed, as Columbia University law professor Eben Moglen told the *New York Times,* it's "spying for free."[1] Advertisers, retailers, and many businesses are busy mining the data, collecting information about us when we're online. Storing a string of text or "cookies" on your computer, companies can track them and get information about your online preferences and purchases, all without your knowing it. Meanwhile, a bill has been drafted in Congress that will require companies to alert consumers when they collect information that could identify them, both online and offline.[2]

PRIVACY IS DEAD: "GET OVER IT"

Privacy issues, obviously, are huge on the Internet, primarily because the surge of use has been happening so fast that there aren't policies in place to handle it and no one anticipated many of the newly surfacing issues. Such policies take time to create, and they tend to develop slowly. "You have zero privacy," the former CEO of Sun Microsystems, Scott McNealy, told a group of reporters in 1999. "Get over it."[3] Sitting there alone in front of a computer or on a cell phone, people have certainly not felt inhibited about sharing details of their lives online, maybe because they can do much of it anonymously. On Facebook, at least initially, it seemed they could control access. Perhaps a loss of privacy is the price for the interconnectivity of the Internet. Online, everyone gives up at least three pieces of information about themselves when they register at a website: zip code, birthday, and gender, all that a third party needs to identify you.[4]

But as high school students, job seekers, and employees have discovered, what happens on the Internet stays on the Internet. College admissions officers, prospective employers, and bosses check Facebook and Twitter postings. Anything posted on Twitter, where people tend to be less discreet, becomes public information, and now it's archived at the Library of Congress and searchable on Google. Eric Schmidt, former CEO of Google, has recommended that teenagers change their names when they reach adulthood to hide their postings from their Google permanent record.[5]

While Twitter users can restrict their accounts, 90 percent still leave their postings open for anyone to access (indeed, Twitter's trending-topics feature wouldn't work at all if everyone designated their accounts as private). Facebook is on the front lines in the battle over privacy on the Internet, revamping privacy settings for its 500 million-plus users (22 percent of everyone online) in order to simplify the way people can block or allow access to their profiles and posts. But critics say this redo has simply made it easier for public search engines like Google and Bing to collect data. Indeed, now that Google Realtime Search will include Facebook profiles and Twitter posts, the issue of what goes public suddenly becomes crucial for all those heretofore heedless oversharers out there. Dylan Casey, Google's product manager for Realtime Search, said in a blog post, "Tweets and other short-form updates create a history of commentary that can provide valuable insights into what's happened and how people have reacted. We want to give you a way to search across this information and make it useful."[6]

Google users can just click "Updates" on a Search page to find Twitter posts for a topic or specific date (or hour). Further, the Library of Congress has now acquired all public tweets in the Twitter archive dating back to March 2006 when Twitter began, a move that will make available to scholars and sociologists a rich source of information about daily life (and consumer preferences).[7]

Social networks like Facebook of course actually encourage users in their postings of personal information, the more the better, as this information can then be sold to marketers and used as a lure for advertisers. In fact, Facebook found itself suddenly embroiled in controversy during the spring of 2010 when it introduced its "Like" button on 100,000 other websites, allowing Facebook users to pinpoint things they like on those websites, which then forward that information to their Facebook pages. Facebook can then keep track of those preferences and use them to pitch advertisers.

Another Facebook program, "Instant Personalization," raised hackles about privacy violations not only among Facebook users but also in the U.S. Senate. This program automatically shares the Facebook information of its 500 million-plus users—profile, photos, friends, gender, whatever else you've posted on your account—with Facebook partners like Pandora and Digg.com unless you opt out, helping these partners to target you for personalized marketing and advertising. The program is controversial because it works by default, and it's complicated to get out of it, according to the *New York Times,* involving clicks on more than 50 privacy buttons and choosing among 170 options.[8] Needless to say, 23 percent of Facebook users either don't know about the privacy settings or don't use them.[9] Most people can't be bothered.

In the Senate, Senator Charles Schumer and others called for an "opt-in" rather than "opt-out" for the privacy feature, and MoveOn.org circulated a petition calling the new Facebook program a major invasion of privacy. Even if a user opts out, his or her friends might not, allowing access to any of the user's private information on their pages. It's already happened; at one point a security loophole on Yelp.com allowed users' data to leak out. Though quickly fixed, the lapse underscored how vulnerable personal data can be online. In another instance, because of a security flaw in Facebook Chat that allowed anyone to see what was being discussed, Facebook had to close down its chat feature temporarily. Meanwhile, an Internet watchdog group, the Electronic Privacy Information Center (EPIC), along with 15 other groups has filed a complaint about Facebook's leaky privacy policy with the Federal Trade Commission.

Facebook's introduction of Facebook Places in August 2010, allowing users to share their location and find their friends, also generated concerns about privacy, with the American Civil Liberties Union (ACLU) in the forefront saying Facebook did not include important privacy features, like being able to opt out of the new location service.[10] Twitter, which introduced a location service earlier the same summer, Twitter Places, has a better opt-out feature, allowing users to choose whether to disclose their location each time they post.[11] A website, Please Rob Me, has sprung up to warn people against giving away their locations, and there's some evidence that location services are not popular.

In yet another instance of threats to privacy, Amazon, the online bookstore that controls 90 percent of the book business, is fighting an attempt by the state of North Carolina to audit all its customer accounts in search of unpaid sales taxes. Amazon said such an audit would be a violation of the First Amendment and customers' privacy rights, arguing that if customers knew that their personal choices (say, *Divorce for Dummies* or *Illegal Drugs: A Complete Guide*), might be surveyed and catalogued by a third party, they would be much less likely to buy books, movies, and CDs from Amazon. In June 2010, Amazon said it would pull its services out of North Carolina entirely.[12]

Four New York University students, in protest of Facebook's privacy policy, decided to build their own social media network, one that wouldn't force users to surrender their data to business and marketers. After several months of successful fund-raising, the group went to work writing code for software they call Diaspora* that will allow users to control their own information and not give it up to "cyber warehouses."[13] Announcing the new network on Twitter, the students quickly amassed several thousand followers, a sign of the dissatisfaction with Facebook out there. In fact, Facebook is the most hated site on the web, ahead even of airlines, cable companies, and the IRS.[14]

According to a survey at the University of California-Berkeley, however, 18- to 24-year-old students have become more concerned about their privacy and Internet behavior, putting a damper on their earlier tendencies to tell all online.[15] A Pew Internet Project study in May 2010 found that students in their twenties were far more likely than younger users to limit and police information about themselves online.[16]

WE ARE BEING WATCHED

Computers and the Internet have made it possible to measure, poll, and survey in thorough and accurate ways never before available or imagined.

While much of the measurement is socially useful and benign, it also exerts control over many dimensions of life not usually subject to such evaluation and gives authority to a reliance on numbers rather than more considered insight. For example, a teacher may be evaluated by the number of her students who pass a test, or the popularity of a Google top-ranked search item by the number of clicks it receives, or a person by the number of followers he or she has on Twitter.

Surveillance cameras are ubiquitous, and after the would-be Times Square bomber was caught on camera in May 2010, New York City police announced they would install 300 more such cameras in that area. We are being photographed constantly and unknowingly every day, on mass transit, at ATMs, standing in line at the bank or grocery store. According to a report by EPIC, the federal government, in the interest of homeland security, provides money to cities to set up their camera networks. Chicago has 2,250 cameras up and running. London has 200,000, one for every 14 people. The average Briton is photographed 300 times a day, according to this report. (New York City Mayor Bloomberg visited to see how the British protect against terrorism.)[17]

The *Wall Street Journal,* in a series of investigative reports in 2010 on "The Web's New Gold Mine: Your Secrets," found that "one of the fastest-growing businesses on the Internet ... is the business of spying." According to the report, 50 of the top websites on the Internet had installed at least 64 pieces of tracking technology on the computers of visitors to the sites, including cookies and more powerful trackers like "flash cookies" and "beacons," which can track where the mouse is moving and what is being typed—with no warning. Some of these tools operate in real time, so they are following you right now, whenever you are on a web page, and are keeping track of you and your expressed preferences for shopping, travel, movies, and whatever else you say. Then they sell it, on "stock-market-like exchanges" where other sites can also buy the data for their own use and to target ads to specific customers.[18]

While the collected information is anonymous, that is, the customer is not identified by name, just numbers, these tracking tools still know everything else you are posting on the web—your zip code and gender, plus estimates of your age, income, marital status, children, home ownership, and even probable vacation plans. Sometimes sensitive health and financial data are picked up this way. The introduction of location services like Twitter Places and Facebook Places only adds to collectable data. The Federal Trade Commission took action against Twitter, prior to its installation of the location service, for serious lapses in its data security, allowing hackers into nonpublic tweets, and for deceiving customers about its security safety. EPIC has asked Congress to update federal law to protect privacy on Facebook and other social media.[19]

Why are we not surprised at all this surveillance and invasion of privacy? The computer and the Internet make online surveillance a slam dunk. Everything is now quantifiable and can be tracked. This kind of customer information is indeed a gold mine for any retailer or business, and a bonanza for sites that sell it, like Lotame Solutions Inc. and IAC/Interactive Corp.'s Dictionary.com, according to the *Journal* article. The U.S. Constitution, in its First, Fourth, and Fourteenth Amendments, covers and protects the right to privacy (the "right to be let alone"—the word *privacy* actually is never mentioned), but in the age of the Internet, the laws on the books are ineffective and not up to date. The problem is that when we give up these data about ourselves voluntarily, on social media networks, blogs, Twitter, and cell phones, we are considered to have given our consent, and present laws do not really protect us. Social media sites have some restrictions in place, and users need to activate privacy options or use one of the networks like Tor, which prevent others from knowing and following online activity. While the U.S. government routinely monitors terrorist groups on the Internet, police and judicial agencies also check Facebook and Twitter accounts. Such surveillance has helped in fighting crime and in jury selection.

Offline, on the now-ubiquitous surveillance cameras, you are not as invisible as you think. You are probably being watched in a dressing room while you try on that new swimsuit, and body scanners at the airport survey your person. You are definitely being photographed as you use an ATM, enter a bank or a grocery store (where data are collected when you use your shopper card), and increasingly on the road, not only with your E-Z pass but when you run a red light or stop sign. Google's Street View cameras have raised plenty of legal issues. Trolling the streets of almost two dozen countries, vans with cameras collect street views for Google Maps and Google Earth, blurring the faces of anyone caught on camera but inadvertently picking up other privacy-threatening information like residential WiFi data, men leaving strip clubs, protesters, and bikini-clad beachgoers. Foreign countries are putting up "No Trespassing" signs, and the European Union has demanded that Google eliminate its photos after six months; Google said it needs to keep photos longer and might have to cancel Street View within the European Union. France called Google a monopoly, South Korea raided Google offices, and Spain and other countries issued subpoenas to stop the roving cameras. In England, Street View was called a "service for burglars."[20]

Walmart is busy attaching new, more powerful radio frequency identification (RFID) chips to the clothing it sells—ostensibly to better monitor inventory and customer preference—but you wind up taking them home with the garment and, at short distance, they can still be tracked (you have to put the garments in the microwave to disable the chip). In three to six years, EPIC estimates, these chips are going to be embedded in everything from groceries to tires, paint cans, exercise equipment, and whatever you buy at CVS. The European Central Bank plans to embed such chips in its currency, allowing a record of each transaction as cash is used and putting an end to the anonymity of using cash instead of a check or credit card.

The question is, how far can this go, and where are we headed as surveillance of all kinds becomes possible in our technology-rich world? It's unlikely, but all this surveillance does have the dark potential to go all the way to an Orwellian *1984* of totalitarian control, and some foreign governments are delighted to have the capacity to monitor their citizenry this way.

ANONYMOUS WAS HERE

Anonymity, of course, is the currency of the web, and it does protect people's identity. Though many prefer to use their own name, plenty of people online take advantage of the anonymity to role-play and adopt new identities or hide behind self-created masks. The protocol of anonymity was set up in the beginning when the structure of the web was created and algorithms were embedded in web software. On Twitter and frequently on blogs, the actual identity of the person posting can be masked by an inventive moniker or fake name. However, while this does protect the blogger or the Twitterer, it also seems to grant license to many users for questionable verbal behavior. Under the cloak of anonymity, feeling uninhibited, people feel free to post nasty, violent, and insulting remarks and make threats and sexual comments. Postings responding to news articles and columnists can be vicious, which is why many sites are now requiring full disclosure of identity before a comment can be posted, which also leads to a higher quality of commentary.

A social-networking site called Formspring.me and connected to Facebook has attracted hordes of teenagers (14 million in the United States alone) as a place for them to gossip and critique others without disclosing their own identities.[21] It goes without saying that the commentary is raw and sometimes witheringly nasty as users discuss other people's looks, lifestyles, and sexual proclivities ("You're not as hot as u think u are").

Just what an insecure middle-school kid needs, cyberbullying. While the Internet has always seemed friendly to transgressive behavior, this is the hive mind gone wild. The number of hate sites on the web has grown 20 percent, according to a report on digital terror and hate sites in 2010 by the Simon Wiesenthal Center, a Jewish human rights group. Attracting terrorists and racists and anybody with an axe to grind, 11,500 hate sites are growing right along with social media.[22]

CYBERBULLYING

Cyberbullying is the schoolyard bully gone viral. It involves repeated, aggressive hostile attacks and harassment of another person online, and it seems to thrive in social media. A 2010 report on cyberbullying by the Pew Internet and American Life Center found that 32 percent of teens between the ages of 12 and 17 reported experiencing some form of cyberbullying. Girls report more online harassment, and those in their midteens, ages 14 to 17, seem to be both the prime victims and aggressors. Though most bullying still takes place at school, the report suggests that the speed of the Internet and the disinhibition of online anonymity add to online bullying.[23] "Sexting," the posting of sexually suggestive photos, particularly on cell phones by older teens, can be a form of cyberbullying.

It is difficult to get definitive cyberbullying statistics, perhaps because teens may be reluctant to admit being the victim or the perpetrator. Another study in February 2010 by the Cyberbullying Research Center, run by Florida Atlantic University and University of Wisconsin professors Smaeen Hinduja and Justin W. Patchin, sampled 10–18-year-olds and found that 20 percent reported experiencing cyberbullying. The report said that girls were more likely to have bullied someone than boys, usually by planting rumors about the other person (boys tend to post offending photos or videos, the study said).[24]

Bullied teens report more depression and school avoidance, and some recent cyberbullying situations have led victims to suicide. A 17-year-old Long Island girl, Alexis Pilkington, killed herself in March 2010 after being repeatedly taunted viciously on social media sites. Even after her death, cyberbullies continued to post nasty messages about her. Phoebe Prince, 15, committed suicide at her home in South Hadley, Massachusetts, in January 2010 following a similar relentless cyberbullying attack. In Missouri in 2006, an adult woman posing as a 16-year-old boy on MySpace cajoled 13-year-old Megan Meier into a relationship, then viciously turned on her with insults and harassment, all apparently over Megan's treatment of the woman's daughter. When Megan committed suicide, the woman was indicted but later acquitted for lack of evidence. While there are bullying laws in Missouri and 43 other states, Missouri's had no cyberbullying provisions, nor do those in all but five of the other states. Cyberbullying provisos are being added to Missouri law and proposed in the U.S. Congress.[25]

What motivates such vicious online bullying? There's a pile-on factor, a mob mentality that is seen in other kinds of bullying. And within the mob, it can be a status thing to join in the scapegoating and victimization of another. Seeking status and approval, a bully at school or online shows off by being the alpha dog of the playground. Psychologically, bullies are said to often be victims of abuse themselves, but some studies show bullies are actually popular kids, not outcasts, who want to raise their social standing by launching these attacks. Sometimes they just want to be noticed. Picking on a safe choice like another child who may already be disliked or scorned (such as Phoebe Prince, who as a newly arrived immigrant from Ireland was already an outsider), a bully can marshal a crowd to help attack the victim and thereby raise his or her own status. The anonymity of the Internet removes inhibition, as in hate sites and the nasty remarks consistently posted on comment boards, and people pile on.[26]

GOVERNMENT MONITORING AND BLOCKING

The explosion of online information and citizen commentary is making foreign governments nervous, especially those that need to keep a tight handle on dissent and stop the rest of the world from finding out about their activities. Blocking or shutting down Twitter, Facebook, and Google and arresting people who speak out, countries with state-controlled media try to stop the social change, criticism, and dissent bubbling out of the Internet and threatening their authority. The United Arab Emirates suspended all BlackBerry service in the country in 2010 because the provider, Research in Motion (RIM), would not redo its systems to let the government intercept the communications of subscribers. India also threatened to block BlackBerry service if RIM did not let law enforcement monitor messages.[27]

The "Enemies of the Internet" list drawn up in 2010 by Reporters Without Borders (Reporters Sans Frontières) shows "the worst violators of freedom of expression on the Net" to be Saudi Arabia, Myanmar (Burma), China, North Korea, Cuba, Egypt, Iran, Uzbekistan, Syria, Tunisia, Turkmenistan, and Vietnam, all of which have attempted to limit, filter, or shut down Internet service. The biggest danger to such governments is the possibility that through the Internet, the citizenry can mobilize against them, which the uprisings in Egypt and other Middle East countries, partially organized online, have shown to be true. Meanwhile, stories of government abuse trickle out as citizens learn ways to evade filters and shutdowns.[28]

Google has introduced a Government Requests tool that shows the number of requests by foreign countries to remove data from Google search results. The data is broken down by whether Google complied with the requests. However, the tool provides little information about what content was taken down and why, an issue Google said it plans to address in the future. Of the data currently available, Brazil made the most requests for data to be removed, which could be linked to Google's Orkut social-networking site, popular in Brazil. Listings are based on requests in 2009, to be updated every six months.

Removal requests include information related to criminal investigations, alleged defamation, hate speech, and impersonation. The list does not include requests to remove child pornography because Google said it automatically does that. Portraying the data release as part of its continued championing of openness of information, Google said this fits into its mission "to organize the world's information and make it universally accessible."[29]

The new Government Requests tool has no figures for requests from China—which otherwise would be at the top of the list—because, Google says, the Chinese consider their censorship requests state secrets, so Google will not release them. Google has been embroiled in an ongoing struggle with the Chinese government, whose censorship of search results—and suspected encouragement of hackers to break into Google's most important systems—finally proved unbearable in January 2010 after four years of harassment. Google withdrew from mainland China to Hong Kong where it could cease censoring results, gaining praise and attention for its decision. Google redirected Chinese users to its uncensored Hong Kong–based site, but people inside China could not see it because of the firewall operated by the government.[30]

In the summer of 2010, Beijing offered a compromise after Google made the first move and said it would stop using an automatic redirect to its uncensored Hong Kong site, google.com.hk (users could take an extra step and use a link). Beijing then agreed to license Google to operate a website, Google.cn, in mainland China. While the license to operate can be revoked at any time, Google regarded the renewal of its license as a victory, though its traffic is far behind the local Chinese search engine, Baidu.

China is the biggest Internet market in the world, with 420 million people online and counting.[31]

China has already blocked Twitter and Facebook from operating but is trying to find some local alternatives, "even as it bolsters mechanisms to police Internet traffic and curb unregulated expression online," according to the *New York Times*. Chinese sites like QC and Sina offer Twitter-style services but are frequently "down for maintenance" or being purged.[32]

COPYRIGHT

The Internet makes it shamefully easy to copy other people's words, music, choreography, scripts, books, articles, pictures, and videos. It all seems to be just sitting there, right on the screen, begging to be borrowed, reappropriated, pirated—and it is, big time. But copyright law has lagged behind the speeding traffic of the information highway. Technically, according to the U.S. Copyright Act, "a copyright protects an original literary, musical, dramatic, choreographic, pictorial or graphic, audiovisual, or architectural work, or a sound recording, from being reproduced without the permission of the copyright owner." What can't be copyrighted: ideas and facts. Copyright belongs to the author of the work. The U.S. Constitution gives Congress the right to enact copyright laws "to promote the progress of science and the useful arts" by giving authors exclusive rights to their works for a limited time.[33]

There is such a thing as "fair use" in the law, implemented to allow scholarship and research, depending on the purpose, and to allow quotation or use of part of an author's copyrighted material, depending on the amount. Meanwhile, whole lead paragraphs routinely get taken out of RSS news feeds all the time, showing up on other online news sites, but it is time-consuming for original sources to track them down and follow up.

The Digital Millennium Copyright Act (DMCA) was enacted by Congress in 1998 to cover some of the new issues that technological advances, primarily the Internet, have raised. It amends the U.S. copyright laws to restrict the making, selling, or distributing of devices that circumvent online copyright protection, like code-cracking devices that illegally copy software or circumvent the antipiracy measures built into it (anticircumvention provision). It also provides a "safe harbor" for online service providers if they promptly take down copyright-infringing elements on their systems.[34]

Infringement or violation of copyright is slightly different from plagiarism, which is taking someone else's words without giving credit and pretending they are your own. Infringement or violation of copyright is the unauthorized use of someone else's words, which is against the law. There is some overlap here, but plagiarism is considered illegal only if it infringes on copyright. Nonetheless, both copyright infringement and plagiarism, as well as outright piracy, are big problems in cyberspace, particularly with the downloading of music. Some writers say they try to avoid using the Internet for research mainly because the plethora of information available can lead to these problems. But many student writers surfing the Internet are not sure what plagiarism is and have few qualms about appropriating material, cutting and pasting at will. Again, because of the Internet, it's fairly easy to detect plagiarism. Sites like Turnitin can screen a piece of writing for its "originality index" and highlight anything that comes from a source uncredited in the work. As noted in chapter 6, there have been some famous cases of literary plagiarism by well-known authors like Stephen Ambrose and Doris Kearns Goodwin, who blamed it on their notes, as well as by new, younger writers, one of whom defended herself by calling plagiarism merely a matter of "mixing."

Libel laws apply online as well as in print and on the air. "Libel," as the *Associated Press Stylebook and Libel Manual* says, "is injury to reputation," and any "words, pictures, or cartoons that expose a person to public hatred, shame, disgrace or ridicule, or induce an ill opinion of a person are libelous."[35] So anything you post online that alleges "crime, fraud, dishonesty, immoral or dishonorable conduct, or stories that defame the subject professionally, causing financial loss either personally or to a business" is actionable in a civil libel suit. The primary defense to a charge of libel is that the facts are provably true. A second defense, absolute privilege, applies only to legislative, judicial, and public and official proceedings and records. The press has a qualified privilege to report matters of public interest, but this is tricky and complicated; using the word *allegedly* doesn't stand up in court when a news report on a crime mentions names, unless this is already a matter of official record.[36]

All of which is to say that there have already been lawsuits over potentially libelous statements made in blogs, on Twitter, and on social media networks. Aside from the suit brought by an ex-model over being called a whore on YouTube, defamation lawsuits can arise even out of the comments pages on blogs and news reports, though a federal judge recently ruled in one case that a Mississippi news station was immune from "cyberlibel" in allowing unfiltered reader comments, citing the Communications Decency Act.[37] Hate sites, like that of blogger Hal Turner, who was convicted in August 2010 and faces a possible 10 years in prison for saying in his blog that three Chicago judges he named "deserved to be killed," are rife with libel. In 2009, the *Baltimore Sun* issued a cease-and-desist order for copyright infringement to blogger Jeff Quinton, who admitted that he overstepped fair-use borders by using five lines out of a *Sun* article in his blog.[38]

The jury seems still to be out on whether a 140-character tweet falls under copyright or libel law because there hasn't really been a test case to establish precedent, though Mark Cuban, owner of the Dallas Mavericks, was fined $25,000 by the NBA over a tweet he posted complaining about the refereeing in a game his team lost.[39] The singer Courtney Love was being sued for defamation by a clothing designer over tweet complaints she posted about how she was billed. The first person to be a defendant in a Twitter libel case, Love settled with the designer before they went to trial in February 2011, paying $430,000 in damages.[40]

Retweets could be treated as a link rather than the repetition of libel, but no court has yet ruled on a case involving retweets. There has been a move to allow tweets and live blogs into courtrooms as a way for reporters to keep up with the legal action, and some newspapers, like the Greeley, Colorado, *Tribune* and the *Cedar Rapids Post* in Iowa, are already being allowed to do that.[41]

Twitter itself, in its terms-of-service agreement, makes clear that anything anyone tweets is the responsibility of that individual, not Twitter. Corporations and businesses may have the most legal exposure, but they try to cover their tweets with disclaimers posted on their profiles, though these are seldom accessed by readers.[42]

There are other legal issues arising in cyberspace. Fake reviews of restaurants, video games, music, and movies are all over the Internet, including Facebook and Twitter. In 2010, the Federal Trade Commission stepped in to stop some deceptive advertising by a California public relations company when it was discovered that some employees were being paid to write positive reviews of iTunes games. New York State Attorney General Andrew Cuomo last year oversaw a settlement with a cosmetics surgery company over its faked reviews on the Internet. He called the settlement "a strike against the growing practice of 'astroturfing,' in which employees pose as independent consumers to post positive reviews and commentary to Web sites and Internet message boards about their own company."[43]

To defend themselves against real but negative reviews by customers, some businesses resort to a SLAPP suit (strategic lawsuit against public participation), intended mainly to censor and silence critics and make them pay for their own legal defense. Such suits are usually dropped once the customer gives up and withdraws the critique. But a 21-year-old Western Michigan University student, Justin Kurtz, set up an entire Facebook page, "Kalamazoo Residents against T & J Towing" (which attracted 14,000 fans), to protest the $118 he was billed by T & J Towing after they towed his car out of a legal parking space. The towing company SLAPPed him with a $750,000 suit, claiming defamation.[44] Kurtz and his lawyer countersued, and Kurtz testified at a state house judiciary hearing to support Michigan legislators drafting an anti-SLAPP law. The towing company eventually accepted an offer of zero dollars to settle the suit after a case evaluation by the court.

FACT VERSUS RUMOR

The website PolitiFact.com keeps a daily "Truth-O-Meter" running on political speech and commentary, tagging the untruths or half-truths it picks up from the media, along with a "Pants-on-Fire" list of blatant lies. While some of the false statements are par for the course in political discourse, some say the Internet is causing a new disregard for the facts in its overload of information. Farhad Manjoo, author of *True Enough: Learning to Live in a Post-Fact Society,* says we've entered a dissonant reality on the Internet where so much undifferentiated information comes at us we find it difficult to sort it out. This "has loosened our grip on what is or isn't true," he says.[45] Because more authoritative mainstream media are in decline, Manjoo says we tend to gravitate to and trust online niches that match our own beliefs, whether they are trustworthy sources or not, just because we agree with them. This "facilitates a closeted view of the world." "Digital manipulation is so effortless, spin, conspiracy theories, myths, and outright lies may get the better of many of us," a kind of "biased assimilation" that lets us "select our reality according to our biases."[46] In a culture of simulation, where "strings of binary code that can be understood by machines ... have deepened the disconnect between what we perceive through our senses—what we see and what we hear—and what's actually going on in the world,"[47] it's no wonder that paranoia, polarization, and propaganda have taken hold or that there is a growing mistrust of the media and established institutions.

TWITTER-JACKING

You can be cloned on Twitter. Plenty of people have been, particularly celebrities, politicians, and sports stars. It's way too easy for someone to open a Twitter account pretending to be you and collect followers. Oprah, for example, has been a particular target, and a fake Twitter account for BP Global Oil opened up in the summer of 2010 to post outrageous remarks about the oil spill in the Gulf. Although Twitter doesn't monitor individual tweets per se, its terms-of-service agreement now has to cover every twist of impersonation and "twitter-jacking" of identity that people can think up, from "name-squatting" to trademark and copyright infringement to setting up an account for a dead person. Twitter acknowledges that parody and role-playing might be the impetus for many fake accounts, but Twitter rules say tweeters must make it obvious with a statement such as "This is a parody" and must use a version of the parodied person's real name.[48]

Identity theft of this kind—or the more sinister, hacked kind stealing your social security, bank, or credit card number—is made easy by the Internet, where shopping and online banking and pay sites carry these numbers. Your passwords could be up for grabs, too. Scams are ubiquitous—have you received your e-mail from Nigeria today, telling you you've just inherited a fortune or won money? (Just send along a check to get the cash that's due you.) Hackers have been selling log-in data for 1.5 million bogus or hacked Facebook accounts on the black market, according to VeriSign's iDefense division, as reported in the *New York Times:* "Criminals steal log-in data for Facebook accounts, typically with "phishing" techniques that tricks users into disclosing their passwords or with malware that logs keystrokes. They then use the accounts to send spam, distribute malicious programs and run identity and other fraud."[49]

The tip-off that your Facebook account may be under siege: too many friend requests at once.

NET NEUTRALITY

Net neutrality or an open Internet is about treating all data on the Internet equally, without service providers giving priority and speed—a fast lane—to one kind of content, like video conferencing (and charging for it), over other kinds, like e-mail. The problem is that those who can afford it would pay for the prioritized, faster service and leave the rest of us in the dust. A proposed deal between Google and Verizon brought this issue to the forefront in late summer 2010, leaving proponents of an open Internet worried about the companies' intent, though both deny there would be any compromise of net neutrality.[50] The Federal Communications Commission (FCC), in favor of net neutrality, proposed regulations requiring Internet service providers to treat all web content the same, but it lacks the legal authority to enforce them. Phone companies like AT&T and cable companies are in favor of having some kind of paid priority services on their more limited broadband wiring (to rein in some broadband hogs like Facebook), while wireless companies, now the dominant platform, want no restrictions.[51]

EIGHT

Inventing the Digital Self

A whole generation of "digital natives" has grown up and started to take the helm of the brave new world now evolving online. Born into it and experienced at negotiating it, they basically have known no other than the viral world and its environs. As a result, they have been socialized differently than earlier generations. "They have spent their entire lives surrounded by and using computers, videogames, digital music players, video cams, cell phones, and all the other toys and tools of the digital age," notes Marc Prensky, originator of the phrase *digital natives*.[1] Right now, the oldest members of this generation, sometimes identified as the Millennials, are just hitting 30. They are the ones who are starting businesses, raising families, running for office, and facing the global crises in this new digital world.

"No one has yet been born digital and lived into adulthood or an 80-year lifespan," note John Palfrey and Urs Gasser in their study of this generation in *Born Digital*.[2] Clearly, everything is going to be different when digital natives are running things.

It already is.

There are dozens of research projects underway to analyze this generation and the way their interaction with the Internet is affecting them and the world around them. Born after 1980, this generation, kindergarten through college, is the first to grow up with ubiquitous information technology. They have spent maybe 5,000 hours reading books but 10,000 hours online, playing video games and posting on social media, and some 20,000 hours watching television.[3] As a result, Prensky says, they "think and process information fundamentally differently from their predecessors." Further, as Maryanne Wolf, professor of developmental psychology at Tufts University, writes in her study of the human brain, *Proust and the Squid,* their brains are probably being changed by these experiences. Just as the human brain managed to adapt from an oral culture to a visual, reading mode when the alphabet came on the scene (and, later, the printing press), so now in the digital revolution the brain, ever flexible, has to reengineer itself to negotiate the new online terrain.

While the human brain is innately structured to rearrange itself and perform new functions, Wolf says, the acceleration of information and instant online access to it is going to produce a "differently wired" generation, one whose ability to understand, judge, and reflect on its experiences will inevitably be affected.[4] The brain may be strengthened as it reorganizes to accommodate information technology and the skills it requires. Or it may be weakened. "In the twenty-first century," Wolf comments, "we are poised to change significantly and rapidly in ways that most of us can barely predict or fully comprehend."[5]

Nicholas Carr, whose new book, *The Shallows: What the Internet Is Doing to Our Brains,* says we're losing ground as the Internet trains us to juggle too many things at once, suggests that it turns us into virtual lab rats with all the repetition and reward being online involves. His 2008 *Atlantic* article, "Is Google Making Us Stupid?" became blog fodder for many months, putting forth the idea that we are losing the ability to deploy the capacity of our minds in a deep, thoughtful way because the Internet demands a much different set of skills.

For example, digital natives like to read—skim—fast, probably spending no more than eight to nine seconds on a website. They prefer the graphics first, then the text. They are used to instant gratification and want their information to be entertaining.[6] From newspapers and blogs to books, digital natives expect media to be interactive, allowing comment, feedback, and revision. New technology is also training digital natives to be multitaskers, of necessity able to keep multiple strands of activity—texting, posting on Twitter and Facebook, surfing the web, watching TV, hooked up to an iPod—going at once (but, studies show, multitaskers are not as productive as they think). Their primary online purpose: entertainment. And they are not very concerned about privacy, making their private lives public and documenting their every move. In the U.S. adult Internet population, half of users are ages 18 to 44.

DIGITAL IMMIGRANTS

Contrast that to the "digital immigrant" (again, Prensky's phrase), the older online population ages 45 to 73 plus who are the other half of the adult online population. They are exploring the online world from a life-long analog experience, used to getting their information from the printed word—newspapers and books—and radio and television. They still do, but the younger baby boomers, ages 45 to 55, are, surprisingly, the major demographic on Twitter, perhaps because it offers easy access to communicating and 140 words are just about the right amount to update yourself (and maybe because boomers have always distinguished themselves as trendsetters). Facebook too is increasingly drawing an older crowd.

Still, it's not easy making the transition to a digital world when you've spent half your life in a different, more linear mode, an analog mode, of acquiring information. Digital immigrants are also used to more reflective ways of comprehending the world. Inventing the digital self requires re-engineering longtime habits of communication and information gathering. Yet, it appears, this generation has taken to the online world quickly, if differently from the digital natives. They write e-mails, and they actually make phone calls on their cell phones (though the average number of apps on smartphones is now about 75). Digital natives, on the other hand, particularly teenagers, rarely use their phones for anything but texting (e-mail is so over), at an average rate of 100 texts a day. But an older group, 18–34 years old, is growing the fastest, writing blogs and the most active on Twitter, whether for personal or business purposes. Digital immigrants have also taken to the Kindle and other e-books though it's a safe bet they're keeping those bookshelves of physical books up at home. The convenience and pricing of e-books are persuasive, however, and now even the public library will lend you an e-book right on your computer.

The second-largest Twitter demographic is the digital-native group of 25- to 34-year-olds, a group that is also growing fast.[7] The picture of current bloggerati shows bloggers are predominantly males in their thirties and forties who are college graduates and relatively well off (though some are currently unemployed). They are for the most part Caucasian, though Latino and African American users are gaining ground. But there are more women on Twitter than men, 55 percent to 45 percent, and they use it more, mostly for personal messages according to a 2010 BlogHer survey.[8] In a 2010 demographic study of Twitter, the media measurement site Quantcast found that only 14 percent of Twitter users were 13 to 17 years old.[9]

It's interesting to note that studies show young adulthood, usually defined as between the ages of 18 and 25, the age group so active in social media, also to be a prime time for self-involvement and narcissism. Researchers at the University of Illinois reported data suggesting that narcissism peaks in young adulthood, "not because of cultural changes but because of age-related developmental trends."[10] San Diego State psychologist Dr. Jean Twenge says there is a "narcissism epidemic" and has recently written a book of the same title, contending that the current generation of young adults appears to have more narcissistic tendencies. She says that there is more emphasis on individualism and that focusing on oneself has become more acceptable in our culture.[11] Although psychologists are not in agreement on this, certainly the popularity of Twitter and social media sites among this age group would seem to support such conclusions.

Sociologists have recently identified "emerging adulthood" (those from age 18 to their late twenties) as a distinct life stage, apart from adolescence and actual adulthood. Professor Jeffrey Jenson Arnett at Clark University says there are several reasons to mark this period off separately: the need for more education to survive in an information-based economy; fewer entry-level jobs; less rush to marry because of the acceptance of premarital sex, cohabitation, and birth control; and young women feeling less rush to have babies because of career opportunities and access to assisted reproductive technology for later pregnancies.[12]

During this emerging-adulthood period, Arnett says, young men and women are more self-focused and intensely involved in seeking identity. Significantly, their brains are still developing. At the National Institute of Mental Health, neuroscientists in a longitudinal study of brain development found that the brain does not fully mature until at least age 25.[13] The regions involved in emotional control and high-level cognition, the prefrontal cortex and the cerebellum, are still developing into the mid-twenties, a situation perhaps inadvertently acknowledged by car rental companies who won't rent a car to anyone younger than 25 anyway.

Even if the idea of an emerging-adulthood stage has its critics and is still under study, it doesn't seem a coincidence that this group is heavily into social media. An age group with this kind of self-involvement and identity issues is one ready-made for the kind of "daily me" activity on social media, with its opportunities for self-expression and interactivity. Mary Madden, senior research specialist for the Pew Internet and American Life Project, says that this group's use of the Internet and social media "takes place at a time in life when there's a lot of attention being paid to self-presentation."[14]

Another study reported in May 2010 by the Institute for Social Research at the University of Michigan showed that there has been a significant decline in feelings of empathy among college students. Analyzing data on empathy among almost 14,000 college students over the last 30 years, the study found the biggest drop in empathy after the year 2000, according to researcher Sara Konrath. "College kids today," she said, "are about 40 percent lower in empathy than their counterparts of 20 or 30 years ago, as measured by the standard tests of this personality trait."[15] Possibly the growing emphasis on the self among this cohort corresponds to a devaluation of other people.

Beloit College in Beloit, Wisconsin, has started issuing a "Mindset List" cataloguing the cultural references of the entering freshman class. For the class of 2014, whose members were born in 1992, the 75-item list notes that this group of students doesn't bother to wear a wristwatch because they can check the time on their cell phones, and few know how to write in cursive. In their minds, phones have never had cords, e-mail is way too slow, computers have always had a CD-ROM disk drive, all text is hyper, and Fergie is a pop singer, not a princess. Other items on the list:

- 10. A quarter of the class has at least one immigrant parent, and the immigration debate is not a big priority unless it involves "real" aliens from another planet.
- 26. Unless they found one in their grandparents' closet, they have never seen a carousel of Kodachrome slides.
- 32. Czechoslovakia has never existed.
- 62. Having hundreds of cable channels but nothing to watch has always been routine.
- 69. The Post Office has always been going broke.[16]

PERFORMING AN IDENTITY

In this new "generation me," people seem to love the opportunity that social media give them to display their connections and followers. More than offering everybody their Warholian 15 minutes of fame, these sites and blogs offer users the chance to ensconce themselves within a network as a go-to personality or guru. It's the high school popularity contest transmogrified to online algorithm. You can jack up your rank on Google (known as PageRank, named after Google cofounder Larry Page) just by embedding plenty of links in your blog, or lure followers and fans to your Twitter and Facebook accounts by controversial remarks. The whole status game is about how many people are in your camp, listed as a friend or follower. You can do what Ashton Kutcher did to get his first million followers on Twitter, announcing on YouTube that he was going to beat CNN to the draw. Starting with just a little over half a million followers, who went to work to help, Kutcher made it to a million in less than a week and proclaimed himself king of the media, showing that "a single force" can go up against a whole network, as he told Larry King (on CNN). A year later he had 5.7 million followers on Twitter, but Lady Gaga (now number one with 9,130,986 followers) and Justin Bieber (number two with 8,500,907 followers) were ahead of him by then.

It's a culture of exposure, where social media seem to invite us to let it all hang out in an orgy of exhibitionism, self-involvement, and confession. People are not only expressing themselves in this new participatory culture but also turning private lives into public ones and creating new identities, constantly negotiating their virtual identities. Identity in the physical, visual body is one thing. Online, it becomes a matter of information, what we tell people about ourselves. While emotion is harder to convey in words online, and body language is absent, those writing online have found ways to set the tone, from cutesy emoticons to over-the-top repetition: "You are sooooooooooooooooo amazing!" "High drama" and "stagey experiments in self-hood" on teenagers' Facebook pages are typical behavior, as author Katie Roiphe notes, writing about "The Language of Fakebook" in the *New York Times*. Postings, she says, can seem "fake and stilted and artificial," probably the result of trying to invent a presentable, if not real, self online: "Facebook is the chatter of a big party, the performance of public cleverness, the facades and fronts and personas carefully crafted, the one honed line . . . in short, the edited version."[17]

Starting with a clever name, people online can assume a completely new persona, masking the real one and instead launching the one they'd like to be. The shy, the nerdy, the unattractive can become a social butterfly or a self-styled expert, and no one is the wiser. As a now-famous *New Yorker* cartoon says, "On the Internet, nobody knows you're a dog."

We learn to *perform* the self in our blogs and tweets and social networks, controlling how we appear to others and suppressing our real feelings to convey an impression we think others may find more acceptable. Erving Goffman, in his book, *The Presentation of Self in Everyday Life,* written way before the Internet came on the scene, discussed the way we try to create a public self. Even in person, he said, we tend to create our "front," "that part of the individual's performance which regularly functions in a general and fixed fashion to define the situation for those who observe the performance."[18] He quotes from sociologist Robert Ezra Park: "It is probably no mere historical accident that the word 'person,' in its first meaning, is a mask. It is rather a recognition of the fact that everyone is always and everywhere, more or less consciously, playing a role."[19]

There's a hunger for fame that social media like Twitter and Facebook seem to satisfy, at least in terms of amassing as big a group of followers and friends as possible and constantly posting to keep them all up to date on your activities. Fame, of a sort, is possible, and for attention junkies, there's nothing better than being famous on the Internet. There are even websites with lists of ways to play the fame game, involving a video camera and lots of free time, or, depending on your proclivities, simply by creating controversy or outrage, as Perez Hilton does. Frequent postings and constant responses will collect the all-important posse, your networked ticket to fame. As Rex Sorgatz, media strategist, advised in a *New York* magazine article, "The Microfame Game," you need to "overshare" with frequent "nano-broadcasts" on Twitter, "stylize" ("be a little weird"), and "persist" in responding constantly to your followers so you too can become, in his words, a "fameball."[20] Like a commodity, you can become a famous brand online, even for the wrong reasons.

**"He's not very exciting in social situations
but on the net he's a wildman."**

© Mick Stevens/The New Yorker Collection/www.cartoonbank.com

This kind of narcissistic fame seeking was addressed some time ago by Christopher Lasch in his book *The Culture of Narcissism.* "Every society reproduces its culture—its norms, its underlying assumptions, its modes of organizing experience—in the individual, in the form of personality." For Lasch, the narcissist is the personality of our time, someone for whom "the world is a mirror," someone who copes in this way with insecurity and "the tensions and anxieties of modern life." The narcissist "depends on others to validate his self-esteem," "cannot live without an admiring audience," and "must see his 'grandiose self' reflected in the attentions of others."[21] While Lasch's theories remain controversial, they do seem to validate behavioral patterns that thrive on social media networks.

The major attraction of social media like Twitter and Facebook, for digital natives and non-natives alike, is having an audience for your tweets and comments. Further, it's free, and expressing yourself for free to a ready audience is darned near irresistible. Plus, nobody's in charge, the gatekeepers are absent, and you can do and say whatever you want. The problem is, what you say will be there forever, archived as a tweet in the Library of Congress, searched by Google, and at the ready for college admissions officers and potential employers to pull up. But now you can hire a team or a website to clean up your act. Facebook itself makes it easy. Though not everyone trusts the method, you can simply click "Hide" on any item you don't want people to see (retrievable if you choose), or keep your Twitter account private just for your followers. The website Yelp.com will remove negative reviews for restaurants, movies, and other performances. Last resort: delete your account.

In some ways, people are more sophisticated because of the Internet than they otherwise would be, say in their own small hometowns. Online, they are being exposed to the wider world and to a wide diversity of people, opinions, and cultures. Social media, in fact, are helping people expand their social interaction with people they would never meet otherwise. According to the Pew Internet report on "Social Isolation and New Technology," those who use the Internet frequently "are much more likely to confide in someone who is of another race." Users who share photos online are more likely to discuss political topics with someone of a different party, the survey found.[22]

INTERNET ADDICTION

If it's morning in America these days, among that age group or not, people are going online first thing out of bed (or maybe still in bed) in the morning, on a cell phone, BlackBerry, netbook, computer, or iPad, checking text messages, RSS feeds, and social networks, getting an update on the news and what the blogs are saying. Last thing at night, the same, and all day long whether on the job, commuting, driving, or at home, checking in online means they are always on. The surge in online use that used to come when people arrived at the workplace is happening by 7 A.M. now. Professionals, soccer moms, and high school students alike admit to this routine. There is the feeling they might be missing something otherwise. The Internet is part of their brain, or, maybe, it is their brain.

There's a dopamine factor and some hormones involved in all this online activity that may be part of the attraction. Researchers say the stimulation and excitement of going online can release adrenaline and a squirt of dopamine that reinforces the habit.[23] This is particularly true of those who like video games, but it can be an effect of the anticipation and satisfaction of going online, and it is reinforcing. Real life can have its boring moments, and people who swear off their online usage talk of being bored without the stimulation.

The Internet takes a toll on heavy users, according to Dr. Elias Aboujaoude, director of the Impulse Control Disorders Clinic at Stanford University. "We're paying a price in terms of our cognitive life because of this virtual lifestyle," he says.[24] Internet addiction is not listed in the *Diagnostic and Statistical Manual of Mental Disorders* (DSM) yet, but there are already rehab facilities for treating it. The major symptom seems to be spending so much time on the Internet that it interferes with daily life.

Like other obsessions such as gambling or shopping, excessive Internet use provides a "rush" experience (that "dopamine squirt") and an escape from stress or problems. The Internet also bestows a sense of control, real or imagined, unlike other areas of life that may not yield to the same oversight. Computer games in particular seem to offer feelings of personal success and satisfaction that life itself doesn't. And the connections and status one can achieve online can also be very gratifying. The problem comes when grades or job performance suffers or a whole former way of life is left by the wayside. Addicts are not just the introverted, socially inept techies; Internet addiction cuts across all the demographics of age, gender, education, and income.

In South Korea, "one of the world's most wired societies," where more than 90 percent of homes have a high-speed Internet connection, a three-month-old baby was discovered dead of malnutrition while her young parents spent every night at an Internet café playing computer games (the father is doing jail time for "negligent homicide," while the mother, already seven months pregnant with a second child, was given a suspended sentence). The South Korean Ministry of Public Administration and Safety reported that the country has nearly a million Internet addicts in their twenties and thirties who have grown up with online gaming and other Internet activities. The government is planning to start rehabilitation centers and counseling for students and the unemployed, who, it says, are the most vulnerable. For an addict in South Korea's 24-hour-a-day Internet cafés, "the line blurs between reality and the virtual world," one South Korean university psychiatrist said.[25]

What are the symptoms of Internet addiction? There is a checklist, like the ones used to self-identify for alcoholism, on the website NetAddiction. com, asking things like "Do you feel preoccupied with the Internet (think about previous online activity or anticipate next online session)?" "Do you feel the need to use the Internet with increasing amounts of time in order to achieve satisfaction?" or "Do you feel restless, moody, depressed, or irritable when attempting to cut down or stop Internet use?" Questions like "Have you jeopardized or risked the loss of significant relationship, job, educational or career opportunity because of the Internet?" point to a major issue about Internet use: whether people are becoming more isolated and antisocial because of it.

WON'T YOU BE MY NEIGHBOR?

According to the Pew Internet report, "Social Isolation and New Technology," done in 2009, the Internet has not caused people to withdraw from society. In fact, the study found that "the extent of social isolation has hardly changed since 1985, contrary to concerns that the prevalence of severe isolation has tripled since then." The Pew study found, however, that 6 percent of the entire U.S. adult population currently does not have anyone "with whom they can discuss important matters or who they consider to be 'especially significant' in their life," a trend the report found "starkly negative."[26]

However, Americans' "discussion networks"—a measure of people's "most important social ties"—have shrunk "by about a third since 1985," from three people to two. But the Pew Internet study found that mobile-phone use and active web participation yielded "larger and more diverse core discussion networks."

In a June 2010 report "Neighbors Online," a Pew Internet Personal Networks and Community survey found that only 43 percent of Americans knew any of their neighbors by name. Twenty-eight percent knew none.

"Users of social networking services, the survey found, are 26 percent less likely to use their neighbors as a source of companionship."[27]

Nonetheless, the earlier 2009 Pew study found that just because someone is a heavy web user, that doesn't mean they remove themselves from traditional social activities like visiting a restaurant or hanging out at a bar on a Friday night. According to the study, web users are "45 percent more likely to visit a cafe, 52 percent more likely to visit a library, 34 percent more likely to visit a fast-food restaurant, 69 percent more likely to visit other restaurants, and 42 percent more likely to visit a public park." Social-networking users "are 40 percent more likely to visit a bar, but 36 percent less likely to visit a religious institution."

YOU, UNPLUGGED

When Twitter went down for several hours on August 8, 2009, it was as if life had come to a complete standstill. It was a denial-of-services attack, meaning attackers tried to max out the service by overloading it with messages or triggering errors in the system. This same attack also affected Facebook. Twitter's fail whale, an image of a whale being hoisted out of the ocean surrounded with red-bird tweets, popped up with a message, "Too many tweets! Please wait a moment and try again." Earlier that summer, the overwhelming response to news of Michael Jackson's death on June 25 instantly doubled the number of tweets on Twitter and had brought it to a temporary halt with fail whale pop-ups. Cofounder Biz Stone called that day "the biggest jump in tweets per second since the U.S. presidential election." Google Search was also temporarily overwhelmed, sending error messages to all search requests about Michael Jackson for fear that a cyberattack was underway.[28]

Twitterati were confused and upset by these slowdowns and outages because they had gotten so involved in posting their 140-word updates, 41 percent of which are found to be what a 2009 Pear Analytics survey calls "pointless babble." Nonetheless, Twitterati are attached to this vehicle of self-expression. Conversational tweets amounted to 37.5 percent of the total, with "pass-along value" content about news of interest only 8.7 percent. Self-promotion made up only 5.85 percent of the tweets, surprisingly (and spam only 3.75 percent).[29]

THE KIDS ARE ALL RIGHT

The web is the Wild West, and parents are upset because they can't control what their kids are doing online. While parental blocks are available, there's something new every minute online that needs screening and screening out. There is also a genuine concern that the virtual world is providing the kind of stimulation and involvement that young developing brains are not yet equipped to handle, creating problems with concentration and focus. Attention deficit disorder (ADD) was established before the Internet took hold, but too much online activity could well be adding to the problem of short attention spans.

President Barack Obama is worried too. Addressing the graduating class at Hampton University in Virginia in May 2010, he said to the students,

> You're coming of age in a 24/7 media environment that bombards us with all kinds of content and exposes us to all kinds of arguments, some of which don't rank all that high on the truth meter. With iPods and iPads, Xboxes and PlayStations, information becomes a distraction, a diversion, a form of entertainment, rather than a tool of empowerment. All of this is not only putting new pressures on you; it is putting new pressures on our country and on our democracy.[30]

While it's true that the Internet is a big diversionary escape hatch for many people, new technology has always raised alarms and fearful predictions. When the railroad came on the scene in the 19th century, a British scientist, Dr. Dionysius Lardner, warned that "rail travel at high speed is not possible, because passengers, unable to breathe, would die of asphyxia." The invention of the telephone provoked Rutherford B. Hayes, U.S. president, to say in 1877, "It's a great invention, but who would want to use it anyway?" Similarly, a Michigan bank president said on the arrival of Henry Ford's Model T, "The horse is here to stay and the automobile is only a novelty—a fad." When television became available in the 1950s, people were afraid that children would be harmed, and Hollywood producer Darryl Zanick warned, "Television won't last because people would soon get tired of staring at a plywood box every night." Even Charlie Chaplin, beloved star of many silent films, pronounced the idea of movies "canned drama" and said that people would much prefer seeing flesh-and-blood actors on stage.[31]

So too with the new digital world. There is plenty of doomsaying and negative reaction to this new technology. In his book about the effects of the Internet on culture, *The Cult of the Amateur,* Andrew Keen warns against digital narcissism and "creating an endless digital forest of mediocrity," including "everything from uninformed political commentary, to unseemly home videos, to embarrassingly amateurish music, to unreadable poems, reviews, essays, and novels." Keen says we need "to protect mainstream media content against the cult of the amateur" where the "user-generated content" of the Internet and social media are creating "a tabloid style gotcha culture" and where "one thoughtless throwaway remark" or "off-the-cuff joke" in the 24/7 news cycle can wreak havoc with a reputation. "Let's not," he argues, "be remembered for replacing movies, music, and books with YOU!"[32] Too late. That has already begun to happen.

Lee Siegel, in his book *Against the Machine,* points out that although the Internet is "a marvel of convenience," with the potential to make life "easier, smoother, and more pleasant," it is also powered by "greed and blind self-interest," where commercial interests are masked in "humanistic values" and "pathological patterns of behavior" like identity theft, obsessions, and sexual abuse are magnified.[33] The Internet, he says, "plays to the lowest common denominator of youth" where "popularity ... is [the] Holy Grail." It "serves the needs of the isolated, elevated, asocial individual" and fosters "a myopic glibness and carelessness."[34] These problems, he hastens to add, are not all the fault of the Internet as much as a direction in our culture that it encourages. "The Internet took hold in the culture only when the culture was ready to give it a home."[35] Siegel says that Malcolm Gladwell's book *The Tipping Point* helped to make the idea of the "packaged self" acceptable as "a product we shape and sell through our performance of what we want other people to think is going on inside us."[36]

Jaron Lanier, author of *You Are Not a Gadget,* argues that the digital design of the Internet, created by the original programmers, has had unintended consequences. The basic principle of anonymity online, he says, encourages people to be less than fully present and elevates the collective "hive mind," "suggesting that a random crowd of humans is an organism with a legitimate point of view." "Every element in the system—every computer, every person, every bit—comes to depend on relentlessly detailed adherence to a common standard, a common point of exchange." The design becomes a structure "by which you connect to the world and other people," and "in turn can change how you conceive of yourself and the world," not necessarily for the better.[37]

But there is good news along with all the bad reviews. People now have access to unprecedented amounts of information at their fingertips. Search engines and encyclopedias make it easy to find what you're looking for. According to a 2009 study by the Global Information Industry Center at the University of California-San Diego, the average American consumes 100,000 words of information and 34 gigabytes on an average day, an increase of 350 percent over the past 20 years, and people are learning to process and engage with this huge surge in information.[38] Research is vastly enhanced and easier using Internet sources. We can move around between searches and links and dig up research material we might never have had access to, all without leaving our desks or making a trip to the library. We can be in touch with long-lost friends and with our closest friends and stay connected, whether on social networks or e-mail. We can watch mindless YouTube videos, television shows, and the latest movies, whenever. We can read the news, listen to music, organize our photographs, and write a novel, all online. The few drawbacks seem a small price to pay for the expanded opportunities the Internet makes possible. Unlike the one-way medium of television, which encourages a passive, couch-potato attitude, the Internet requires interactivity, a back-and-forth of dialogue and involvement. In some ways a short attention span is a necessity just to juggle what's coming at you on the Internet.

And according to a Pew Internet study in 2010, "Future of the Internet IV," three out of four experts say that use of the Internet actually "enhances and augments human intelligence,"[39] though it is also training us to fragment our attention and favors the sharpening of our visual prowess over more considered judgment. The information glut has a tendency to fragment knowledge as well. We're satisfied to uncover bits and pieces but not the context or the major work.

Still, two-thirds of the same group of experts said use of the Internet "has improved reading, writing, and rendering of knowledge," according to Janna Anderson, the co-author of the study. Anderson says she sees signs that we are developing "fluid intelligence—the ability to find meaning in confusion and solve new problems, independent of acquired knowledge."

In terms of what the Global Information Industry Center study calls "information time," Americans still watch television for 41 percent of it, but computer activity including games, texting, mobile devices, social media, and watching videos consumes 24 percent, with the remaining information-gathering time coming from radio (commuting time), print media, movies, and music. Though the study shows old media still predominate, the authors predict that by 2015 information consumption "will be considerably changed," with rapid growth online and the advent of mobile television and video over the Internet. While the study showed that most people spend only eight or nine seconds on most Web pages, cycling quickly through, the amount of reading required for information consumption has actually increased.[40]

GOING ROGUE

The built-in anonymity and masking that the online world allows is also a temptation, seeming to allow all kinds of bad behavior. Discussion on the Internet can turn into a "barroom brawl" as William Grueskin, dean of academic affairs at Columbia's journalism school describes it.[41] Indeed, the anonymity of the Internet is "disinhibiting," as authors Palfrey and Gasser say, spawning aggression and some pathologies and addictions.[42] In digital disguise, it's much easier to diss someone else online and say nasty things to them.

Comment streams often become polluted with vicious and vulgar postings, so much so that many bloggers, celebrities, and commercial brands now require anyone who wants to comment on their post to reveal his or her real name. This, they say, has cut down on the "sock puppetry" of anonymous and nasty commentary and increased the quality of debate and discussion.

To prevent flame-infested posts, the *Wall Street Journal* site allows readers to select only those comments written by subscribers, whose posts might be thought to be more dedicated. Other sites simply don't allow comments. Scott Rosenberg, cofounder of *Slate,* says what's needed is more supervision: "If you opened a public cafe or a bar in the downtown of a city, failed to staff it, and left it untended for months on end, would you be surprised if it ended up as a rat-infested hellhole?"[43] Even in China, the State Council is pushing a requirement that all 422 million Internet users must use their real names to post and purchase.

Some website proprietors, recognizing that outrageous remarks and comments can boost views, actually encourage them. One website, Formspring.me, allows users to sound off anonymously without restraint with opinions and critiques of people they know, to cruel and detrimental effect. It has become the new place for teens (and grown-ups) to hang out, gossiping and commenting on each other's foibles ("You look stupid when you laugh," "How far did you go with Brad?"). Users can link the site to their Twitter or Facebook accounts and invite their friends to join in, all anonymously. Twenty-eight million people have visited this site, 14 million of them in the United States,[44] though there's no count of what percentage are teenagers on Twitter.

Like Honesty Box, a Facebook add-on, Formspring can also harbor cyberbullies, a new field of endeavor for your standard bully or mean girl, made possible by the Internet and its anonymity. Cyberbullying has led to severe consequences. The suicide of Massachusetts teen Phoebe Prince and of other victims is said to be a result of the relentless attacks that the Internet allows bullies to launch; unlike in a schoolyard, the attacks can go on online 24/7.

Negative and thumbs-down comments about a brand or a business are easy to make online, and customers are quick to post their opinions and reviews, good and bad. Now businesses are trying to fight back. A towing company in Kalamazoo, Michigan, sued a customer who posted a negative review of the firm on Facebook, saying he had defamed them with his venting. "The only thing I posted was what happened to me," said the college student, Justin Kurtz, whose legally parked truck was towed.[45] First Amendment lawyers say many businesses file against people who speak out against them. The website Yelp.com, like Facebook and Twitter, offers to let customers vent their complaints against brands and businesses (which has increased the number of lawsuits) but will also remove an especially negative review.

THE CULTURE OF THE iGENERATION

While it's too soon to know where all this is leading to, it's clear not only that the culture is changing but also that, living in it, we ourselves are being transformed by our interaction with the technology of the Internet. An entire generation is now growing up in front of a browser, as Chris Anderson, editor of *Wired,* has noted.[46] They have known no other and have not yet fully achieved the markers of adulthood—marriages, mortgages, children, and career success are still to come—or lived to a ripe old age. They haven't written the novels that will be the e-books of the future or created the art or music or films that will reflect their sense of the world, though they're working on it. They don't have power in government but are already challenging those who do with their own forms of bottom-up power. Stick around.

NINE

Bloggerati, Twitterati, and the Transformation of Practically Everything

CULTURE GOES VIRAL

The 21st-century culture emerging from blogs, Twitter, and all the activity on the Internet is still taking its baby steps. It's not clear what it will grow up to be or what the culture will look like when it does. One thing is clear: American and global culture are changing faster than anybody can really keep track of. The pace of change is exponential, riding a rocket, with technology and the Internet as the major change agents of unprecedented transformations still to come.

Now that even Tasmania, a little island off the coast of Australia, has laid fiber-optic cable to provide broadband for all of its 500,000 citizens—at speeds 20 times faster than the rest of us get[1]—we have to acknowledge that the revolution has indeed arrived and gone global. The game has changed.

Will we all turn into cyborgs, Donna Haraway's metaphor of what happens to human beings in cyberspace, part human, part machine?[2] Will robots take over the housework and cut the grass? Is artificial intelligence (AI) about to make humans obsolete? Will the Singularity really come to pass by 2030 and take over the world?

It's not just science fiction. But let's take it down a notch or two, down to where we're living right now. Already we've made huge changes in the way we communicate and engage with each other, thanks to the Internet. We're back in touch with high school buddies and long-lost relatives, and we can get information on just about anything and say just about anything we want online. We're always on, multitasking, stress level high, thanks to a handy smartphone that we hardly ever use for an actual phone call. Not spending a whole lot of face time with our near and dear either, but we keep up on Twitter. We may not do much reading, but we own a Kindle. And we may not read a newspaper anymore, now that the news comes through online for free.

Our lives have changed dramatically, not just because we are online but because the whole world is going online, to the tune of more than 1.9 billion people in 2010, or 28.7 percent of the world's 6.8 billion population. The top 10 languages on the Internet are English (the global language), Chinese, Spanish, Japanese, Portuguese, German, Arabic, French, Russian, and Korean. Asian countries, particularly China and Indonesia, have taken to the Internet big time, with 825 million people online, 21.5 percent of the population. Europe has the second-highest count of Internet users, at 475 million, 58 percent of its population. North American users come in third, with 266 million on the Internet, but that represents a whopping 77.4 percent of the population. Surprisingly, Australia and surrounding Oceania, population 35 million, already have 21 million of that population online.[3] By comparison, 10 years ago in December 2000, there were just 361 million people worldwide using the Internet.

Do the math. From 361 million people online in 2000 to 1.9 billion in 2010 is a 444.8 percent increase. We're all going viral at record pace, assisted by the ubiquity of mobile devices in this country and abroad (especially in Africa, where cell phones fill in for the lack of computers). What's emerging is a culture marked by a kind of hyperconnectivity and interaction never before experienced. It's consciousness altering. Where are we headed, and what is that culture going to be like?

Nobody knows yet.

But plenty of critics are thinking and writing about it. *Harper's* editor Bill Wasik, in his recent book *And Then There's This,* talks a lot about the herd mentality that is developing online and the "state of permanent distraction" we're in as a result of hours spent clicking around the web. He brings up an important aspect: "What the Internet has done to change culture—to create a new, viral culture—is to *archive* trillions of our communications to make them linkable, trackable, searchable, quantifiable, so they can serve as grist for yet more conversation."[4] We're creating our own cultural legacy in tweets, blogs, and social media, and we're sending it out around the world. It's all in the Library of Congress, searchable on Google.

Wired columnist Clive Thompson suggests that we're developing an "ambient intimacy" with our friends and followers on Twitter and

Facebook, a relationship that is sometimes better online than in person but that is also more of a milieu of friendship, without the giveaway of body language that might send a different message. The term *ambient intimacy* is oxymoronic: being close in a distant sort of way. Thompson mentions a sociological term, *ambient awareness,* to describe our online modus operandi, picking up clues "out of the corner of your eye." Both terms suggest the way a fast, online environment is retraining us socially.[5]

That astute observer of all things cultural and literary, critic Michiko Kakutani of the *New York Times,* suggests that meeting up with the Internet is the best thing that ever happened to postmodernism, that remixer of culture that has come into its own, feeding on the fragmentation of data and mashing up everything in sight at wicked speed. In the playful, pseudoworld of the Internet, "our cultural landscape is brimming over with parodies, homages, variations, pastiches, collages, and other forms of 'appropriation art'—much of it facilitated by new technology that makes remixing, and cutting and pasting easy enough for a child," and "running the gamut in quality." The web, she says, amplifies subjectivity with its "self-dramatizing blogs" and the daily me of social media.[6]

Jaron Lanier, author of *You Are Not a Gadget,* says that the "most obvious aspect of digital culture" is that it is "comprised of wave after wave of juvenilia," noting the online adolescent atmosphere and "playhouse" ambience of social networks. Even computer engineers can be found sending each other "little digital pictures of teddy bears and dragons."[7] It's like recess for grown-ups. The "youthiness" of the web is hard to resist, apparently.

However, influential blogger Steve Rubel, a public relations executive, says, "It's time to prepare for the end of the Web as we know it." Internet consumption with short attention spans is shifting to gadgets and an app world, where "content snacking" and "infinite choice" prevail. "Mobile devices put all of this in our pockets," and information needs to be repackaged "for an entirely different modality than platforms of yore." The "grandiose design and complexity" of the web "will fall by the wayside."[8]

Similarly, Chris Anderson, editor of *Wired,* and journalist Michael Wolff have announced "The Web Is Dead, Long Live the Internet." "The notion of the Web as the ultimate marketplace for digital delivery is now in doubt" for commercial interests, they claim, driven instead by apps (applications) rather than web browsers. The noncommercial, creative user prefers app-dedicated platforms that are right there on the screen of the smartphone or iPad. "They use the Net, but not the Web—it's all about getting, not browsing." The real revolution is the Internet, Anderson and Wolff say, "as important as electricity," but "what we do with it is still evolving."[9]

Perhaps there is no better sign of the times than the emergence of out-every-night social media consultants like a 38-year-old named Rex Sorgatz, a microcelebrity of the new-media world with spiked red hair, a five o'clock shadow, and blazer-thrown-over-T-shirt style. Good at gaming the system, Sorgatz wrote an article, "The Microfame Game," for *New York Magazine* when he first arrived in New York City, setting out the rules of becoming "microfamous" and "closing the gap between devotee and celebrity." Create controversy, he advises, and collect a posse around you. Sample commentary: "The dirty little secret of so many social-media and-networking sites, including Facebook, Flickr and FriendFeed, is that they disguise self-publicity and oversharing as chatting with friends and uploading storage."[10] Needless to say, Sorgatz himself is "microfame" worthy. Toting his iPad and iPhone 4, Sorgatz can be spotted in Twittered-about New York City hot spots helping to launch a new website or restaurant in his role as marketing guru and digital-media strategist. (Sorgatz has a blog, *Fimocuolus,* http://www.fimoculous.com)

A NICHE CULTURE

While we can talk of some homogeneity, digital culture is actually splintering, fragmenting into a million different niches. There is so much choice that everyone can find a niche and an audience of the like-minded to hang out with online. We can find our tribe and settle in—which is exactly what Marshall McLuhan predicted would happen as technology took over. The tribes of the web are numerous, having coalesced around sites of ideology and politics, celebrities, gossip, fashion, gender, and more, wherever they feel at home. What they have in common is digital culture.

We've moved from the linear, sequential world of print to the postprint world of the binary bit, where information goes digital, translated into numbers, complex combos of bits that at their simplest are the either/or of "on" and "off," or 0 and 1, and moving at the speed of light. As Massachusetts Institute of Technology professor Nicholas Negroponte puts it, bits are "the DNA of information," where a binary code of 0 and 1 can represent the numbers 1,2,3,4,5,6,7 and so on, just with numbers that have 0 and 1 in them: 1,10,11,100,101,110,111. These are the strings of numbers that get organized into a computer language like Java or BASIC.[11] Computer or programming language has syntax, as does regular language, but its words have precise definitions, unlike the changing meanings of words in ordinary language. It is an artificial language written for a machine.

Computer science is all about this kind of encoding, rendering the analog world of human experience as a digital, numerical one, an arbitrary language where information is much easier to store, copy, and transmit. Think of it as the difference between an analog clock where time can be shown in its continuity as it unfolds in all its increments, and a digital clock that can pinpoint the exact time but not its continuous progression. The digital world is discontinuous, made up of discrete and finite numerical digits (the word *digit,* from the Latin *digitus,* means finger or a number).

But actual human experience, let us note, is not digital but analog, a continuous stream of consciousness and sensory input. Sight, voice, and hearing are analog, that is, registering variable physical qualities; so is music and every other art. CDs must convert their binary codes back to analog sound waves to be heard. The digital world is basically a binary one, having two parts, true and false, either/or, up or down. Even though it is an electronic transmission and storage system, as more and more of our experience translates into computer code, things valuably human may be left out or marginalized. The computer can't identify metaphor, for example, or write poetry or music, or feel emotion. Computers don't do nuance. They are powerful and efficient, but their digital language, essentially abstract and reductionist and written for a machine, is irrevocable and unstoppable. As more and more of our daily life is spent online and alone in a digital world, "our perceptions and sensitivity to human meaning may be altered," as Negroponte says in *Being Digital.*[12]

CYBERCULTURE

In our ethnographic thick description of digital culture in this book, this much is clear:

- Blogs are thriving, though personal blogs are gradually moving to social media. But social media have not killed blogging, which has become "the center of gravity for in-depth, substantial dialogue and inquiry online," Scott Rosenberg, cofounder of *Salon.com,* says.[13]

- Twitter, the online water cooler, is growing and evolving. Its role as first responder to world events is well established, making it a news platform as well as a social media network.

- We are more connected and involved in more dialogue with more people in our lives than ever before, even as we are mostly alone as we do this and may neglect face-to-face personal relationships.

- This circle of friends and acquaintances is more diverse and international than ever before.
- We are able to express our opinions, thoughts, and feelings as fully as we like, without editors or gatekeepers.
- Information and ideas are coming from the bottom up, produced by ordinary people, not just the established tastemakers and experts.
- Yet we gravitate to the people, blogs, and websites that support our own views, and our view of the world is becoming more polarized ideologically.
- The world population on the Internet is beyond counting, but an elite group of young, white, affluent, well-educated people dominate certain areas such as blogging, Twitter, and social media.
- The digital divide is generational as well as geographical and financial. The split between younger digital natives and an older generation is wide but likely to close, as 55-year-olds and up discover the advantages of being online. Efforts to expand broadband access will be supported and succeed, but there will be skirmishes ahead over net neutrality.
- Blogging has effected major change in politics and journalism; blog sites like the *Huffington Post* and the *Daily Beast* will become full-fledged online newspapers.
- The Internet has been cost-free for its entire life of 41 years. Putting up paywalls around media websites is going to be difficult.
- Traditional print newspapers and magazines will go digital or go out of business.
- Citizen journalists will continue to report breaking news. Professional journalists will continue to go online or go freelance.
- Mobile devices like the iPhone and the iPad and innovative new devices will leave the computer behind to be used only in offices and schools.
- Google TV announced that the web will soon be coming to your living room TV.[14]
- Books will go digital big time. Bookstores will become publishers or boutique operations or go out of business. Publishers will produce e-books, not print books, or go out of business. Self-publishing will surge as everybody and his brother writes and self-publishes a book.
- Many longtime, established businesses will close: mapmakers, music and record stores, credit card companies (money is going digital too), advertising agencies, even the post office.

- In becoming a digital self, people perform the self they want to be. The element of masking and impersonation that online social life allows is seductive.

- Kids are going to be more knowledgeable, at least about where to get information. Their knowledge quotient might be something else. Digital natives experience the world in a less linear, chronological way, clicking around the web and multitasking. Educating them in the old, linear classroom is going to be a challenge.

- Language is changing in the public space as a streetwise vernacular becomes acceptable. But online, people are doing much more reading and more writing than they used to.

- The privacy of a more individualized focus, one that the printing press and the book fostered, is being compromised and invaded. The younger generation seems not to worry much about privacy as they make public their inner lives.

- Businesses and advertisers have found the holy grail in social media where they can collect information about consumers and target ads directly to them. The "Like" button conveniently helps collect it, and it's no wonder Facebook is trying hard to get people to disclose personal information—that's how they make money.

- Politics will be a whole new ballgame in the next presidential election because of blogs, Twitter, and social media networks.

- The economy will change because of the Internet, which so far has tended to enhance productivity. Late capitalism is morphing into new capitalism as the Internet connects and unifies, improving efficiency and widening communication globally. There are new forms of production like "open-source" methods, where groups of people all over the world can develop products collectively,[15] and companies can use "crowd-sourcing," inviting input from the online public on things like developing a new business or product.[16]

- The stock market will change. It is already faster with electronic communications networks, and it is subject to more global influence because of the Internet. Automated computer strategies can execute trades in milliseconds.

SOME PREDICTIONS

What can be predicted about the shape of American and global culture for the immediate future? Eric Schmidt, former CEO of Google, made these predictions in the fall of 2009 about what the Internet will look like five years from now:

- The Internet will be dominated by Chinese-language content.
- Today's teenagers are the model of how the Web will work in five years—they jump from app to app to app seamlessly.
- Five years is a factor of ten in Moore's Law, meaning that computers will be capable of far more by that time than they are today. *(Author's Note: Moore's Law, as suggested in 1965 by the cofounder of Intel, Gordon Moore, is that the density of transistors on the integrated circuits or chips of computers will double approximately every two years, meaning an increase in speed and memory, and in the number of pixels on digital cameras.)*
- Within five years there will be broadband well above 100 MB in performance—and distribution distinctions between TV, radio, and the web will go away.
- Content will move towards more video.
- Real time, social information needs to be included in search results, but how do we rank it? (How to rank one tweet ahead of another?)
- It's because of this fundamental shift towards user-generated information that people will listen more to other people than to traditional sources, but "the great challenge of the age" is learning how to rank this content.[17]

Other predictions:

- Cloud computing, using distant servers for data storage and management with software coming from the servers, is the next wave. On demand, like electricity.
- Web 3.0 is next, "applications that are pieced together"—with the characteristics that the apps are relatively small, the data are in the cloud, and the apps can run on any device (PC or mobile), are very fast and very customizable, and are distributed virally (social networks, email, etc).[18]
- The personal computer will get smaller, maybe even vaporize, hiding away instead in everyday objects like a pen or an earring, as Silicon Valley develops a new generation of tiny switches called "memoristors" that can hold as much data as a whole disk drive.[19]

- American popular culture is going worldwide and viral on the Internet. There will be more homogeneity but also more subcultures. Pop culture will be governed less by blockbuster hits than by niche hives.

- Blogs, Twitter, and social media will continue to be the venue of self-expression and the vehicles of breaking news and influential opinion in an ever-more-democratized culture. Facebook wants to take over the web. New social media networks will arise and challenge it.

- Popular culture, archived in blogs and Twitter and other social media, is searchable and measurable.

- People will be more knowledgeable, though not necessarily wiser.

- But there will be a proliferation of bad information, rumor, and false-hoods.

- There will be more cybercrime and hacking.

- The power structure will change, breaking the grip of established institutions on culture and giving more power to the ordinary person. This turns on its head Karl Marx's famous pronouncement that the class that owns the means of material production also has control over the means of mental production. Increasingly on the Internet the means of mental production are in the hands of users. But they are still subject to powerful forces that control the structure of the Internet.

- It will be harder to take over the world because the Internet gives a voice to individuals and protest can be organized more quickly and efficiently.

- Privacy on the Internet is essentially over. But surveillance of our personal and private lives will increase because the Internet makes it so easy. One California school wants to tag its preschoolers with radio frequency identification chips (RFID) so it can keep track of them.[20] In China, anyone who wants to buy a SIM card (calling card) for a cell phone has to present identification, a regulation, analysts say, that just makes it easier for the government to censor unacceptable calls.[21]

- Everything that can go digital will: news, money, credit, postage, votes.

- People are dividing along the new fault line of personal choice the Internet makes possible, rather than circumstances like race or wealth. They find support for their choices online (homeschooling, knitting groups, online dating, etc.).[22]

- More people will work at home.

- Women will dominate social networks. They already make up 50 percent of the population on Facebook, and they spend more time there than men do. Women purchase 85 percent of consumer goods, and 22 percent of women now shop online.[23]
- Smarter kids, harder to educate. Their attention span has adapted to a discontinuous mode of collecting information, and their respect for authorship and sources has been eroded.
- A streamlined Main Street: fewer stores but an online presence.
- An increasingly isolated individual within the nuclear family.
- Identity will be decentered and multiple. "When your words or actions or art are available not only to your friends but to potentially thousands or even millions of strangers, it changes what you say, how you act, how you see yourself," *Harper's* senior editor Bill Wasik observes.[24]

There are more drastic predictions: "E-mail is dead," according to Sheryl Sandberg, chief operating officer of Facebook. "The Web is dead": Chris Anderson, editor of *Wired.* "Privacy is dead": Scott McNealy of Sun Microsystems. "The computer is over": Steve Jobs of Apple. "Paper is going away": Nicholas Negroponte, Massachusetts Institute of Technology.[25]

HOW I LEARNED TO STOP WORRYING AND LOVE THE INTERNET

Generally speaking, the more information and knowledge a society has, the more advanced it is, according to sociologist Gerhard Lenski, who posits technology and economics as the major determinants of cultural evolution.[26] Yet a culture drowning in information as ours is now doesn't yet really have the capacity to manage and use it to advantage. Critics contend that real knowledge is being weakened and fragmented by the assault of information we're subjected to online. Facts get slippery in such abundance, and rumors and propaganda take root. Even the Google Books project of scanning every book in every library into a database won't give us knowledge.

We are living in a different world now, a virtual world to a large extent. If, as Clifford Geertz says, "Culture is a context," ours is an unprecedented, unstable, and shifting context. As Sherry Turkle says in *Life on the Screen,* quoting anthropologist Victor Turner, we are in "a liminal moment," on a boundary between the real and the virtual, a time of "tension, extreme reaction, and great opportunity." Surrounded "with predictions of doom and predictions of imminent utopia," we are learning to live with contradictions that are not yet resolved and won't be for some time.[27] In his book *The Crack-Up,* novelist F. Scott Fitzgerald described this situation as a test, "the test of a first-rate intelligence," which is "the ability to hold two opposed ideas in the mind at the same time and still retain the ability to function."[28]

It's the new normal.

TEN

Welcome to the Revolution

Author Gary Shteyngart pictures our future in his novel, *Super Sad True Love Story,* where everybody in New York City wears an "apparat" around their necks, constantly in digital touch with what's happening and streaming their own activities out to the Net.[1] The novel's 39-year-old hero, Lenny, writes a blog diary throughout, worrying about his "Ohio-shaped bald spot," getting older, and holding on to the new love he met in Rome, 24-year-old Korean American Eunice Park of Fort Lee, New Jersey. In contrast to Lenny's old-style lengthy, ruminative blogs, Eunice texts him in cryptic cyberspeak. As the pair walk the streets of the city, their credit ratings, health status, and "hotness" scores are digitally flashed on street poles as they go by. In Central Park, a government army controls a riot by strafing in a helicopter, shooting at random. The Chinese have taken over America, and the dollar is now yuan-pegged.

Grim, but just one of many scenarios spawned by the digital revolution that's sweeping the globe. Everything is changing, and we're right in the middle of it. No one really knows where we're headed and what the outcome will eventually be. Artists, the "antennae of the race," as poet Ezra Pound called them, have been trying to tell us for years what's coming. The Whitney Museum Biennial has been filled with computer art in show after show. Artist Jenny Holzer's digital messages—"technology will make or break us"—have flashed at us on the Times Square news crawl and on the facades of buildings, including St. Patrick's Cathedral. William Gibson's cyberpunk novels like *Necromancer* are starting to seem less like science fiction and more like possibilities. Even Hollywood's apocalyptic films seem more realistic than they used to.

The Singularity Institute for Artificial Intelligence in Silicon Valley is an organization devoted to the idea that the acceleration of technological progress will produce a singular event that will change everything. The institute, generously supported by Google, says we are entering "an era in which our intelligence will become increasingly nonbiological and trillions of times more powerful than it is today—the dawning of a new civilization that will enable us to transcend our biological limitations and amplify our creativity."[2] By 2030, spokesman Raymond Kurzweil says, humans and machines will merge and "transcend all the limitations of our biology."[3] Kurzweil, who invented a computer that composed music when he was 17 and later came up with a print-scanning device that converts text to audio and allows the blind to read, predicts that technological progress in the 21st century will be 1,000 times greater than that in the 20th. By 2030, we'll be able to back up our brains, regenerate organs, and live hundreds of years.[4]

With less dramatic pronouncements, the Pew Internet and American Life Project, reporting in 2010 on "The Future of the Internet IV," polled technology and media gurus for their forecasts about what the Internet will look like by 2020. A sample:

> "More-powerful mobile devices, ever-cheaper netbooks, virtualization and cloud computing, reputation systems for social networking and group collaboration, sensors and other small systems reporting limited amounts of information, do-it-yourself embedded systems, robots, sophisticated algorithms for slurping up data and performing statistical analysis, visualization tools to report results of analysis, affective technologies, personalized and location-aware services, excellent facial and voice recognition, electronic paper, anomaly-based security monitoring, self-healing systems—that's a reasonable list to get started with. Beyond five years, everything is wide open."
>
> —Andy Oram, editor, O'Reilly Media

> "The ability to connect to the web becomes ubiquitous. It will become commonplace to be able to overlay reviews of a product simply by pointing a screen at it, or check the weather forecast by pointing your phone at the sky."
>
> —Rich Osborne, web innovation officer, University of Exeter.

> "By 2020 we will see next generation 3D HD Display technology, coupled with multi-modal sensor input application integration. This will include HDTV which can recognize and understand the viewers

using multi-modal (sight, sound, speech, touch) and services which help manage and personalize media."

—William Luciv, managing director,
Viewpoint West Partners LLC

"It takes a generation, about 25 years, for the new 'thing' to really have its impact. At first society uses the new tool to better do what they have been doing. The generation raised with it finds totally new things and ways to do things. Thus we will be working in jobs that we cannot now see or define."

—Ed Lyell, former member Colorado State Board of Education
and Telecommunications Advisory Commission.[5]

The Pew report found that the panel of technology experts (81 percent) thought that the Internet would enhance people's intelligence by 2020, not make them dumber (referring to Nicholas Carr's article, "Is Google Making Us Stupid?" in the *Atlantic*). "As people have unprecedented access to more information, they will become smarter and make better choices."[6]

BLACK SWANS AND ROUGH BEASTS

The outlook for the future of the Internet seems exciting and hopeful. Yet one author, Nassim Nicholas Taleb, warns in his book, *The Black Swan,* of unforeseen crises (black swans) that can and do disrupt human history, for example, "the natural tendency of networks"—assemblages of elements called nodes that are somehow connected to one another by a link, as are airports, the World Wide Web, social connections, and electricity grids— "to organize around an extremely concentrated architecture." "Random insults to most parts of the network will not be consequential since they are likely to hit a poorly connected spot." But it also makes networks more vulnerable to Black Swans, "especially if there is a problem with a major node," as we have seen in electricity blackouts, in the financial meltdown of 2008, and on the Internet. Taleb says black swans have three main qualities: They are unpredictable, they have a massive impact, and, afterward, we tend to view them as less random and more predictable than they were. Black swans are not all bad, but they can be devastating in other ways. For example, Google was a black swan, but so was 9/11. Black swans can open up opportunities as well as shut them down.[7]

Irish poet William Butler Yeats described an ominous future in his poem, "The Second Coming": "What rough beast, its hour come round at last, slouches toward Bethlehem to be born?"[8] A question the Internet doomsayers ask, though not so elegantly.

The year 1984 came and went, and George Orwell's predictions in his novel, *1984,* did not come to pass. Nor did Y2K, the millennium turnover on computers that was supposed to shut the world down, amount to anything. The future, as always, remains clouded. The pace of change is so swift that this microhistory of digital culture, midrevolution, can only report on the right now, the Twitter-like "what's happening," and only guess at what form our culture will take. As Professor Ray Browne, the founder of the academic discipline of popular culture studies who is often credited with coining the term, has said, "Popular culture is one of the most changeable aspects of our way of life. Literally here today and gone tomorrow. Popular culture is never static but always dynamic." It is, he said, "the voice of the people—their practices, likes, and dislikes—the lifeblood":

It is the everyday world around us: the mass media, entertainments and diversions. It is our heroes, icons, rituals, everyday actions, psychology and religion—our total life picture. It is the way of living we inherit, practice, and modify as we please, and how we do it. It is the dreams we dream while asleep.[9]

He could have been talking about the Internet.

Notes

CHAPTER 1

1. McLuhan, *Understanding Media: The Extensions of Man.* New York: McGraw Hill, 1964.

2. Rich, "'Mad Men' Crashes Woodstock's Birthday," *New York Times,* August 16, 2009, WK8.

3. Quoted in Frank James, "Jet Blue Acknowledges Steven Slater Incident," *The Two-Way,* August 11, 2010, http://www.npr.org/blogs/thetwo-way/2010/08/11/129132386/jetblue-steven-slater-flight-attendant.

4. Wasik, "Bright Lights, Big Internet," *New York Times,* July 30, 2009, A31.

5. Apple Inc., "Apple Reports Third Quarter Results," July 20, 2010, http://www.apple.com/pr/library/2010/07/20results.html.

6. World Internet Usage, http://www.internetworldstats.com, August 30, 2010.

7. Negroponte, *Being Digital* (New York: Alfred A. Knopf, 1995).

8. Quoted in Aimee Lee Ball, "Reflections in the Facebook Mirror," *New York Times,* June 20, 2010, ST2.

9. "Online Hate Sites Grow with Social Networks," *New York Times, Bits Blog,* March 16, 2010, http://bits.blogs.nytimes.com/2010/03/16/online-hate-sites-grow-with-social-networks.

10. "Social Networking Websites More Popular Than Porn Says Study," *Telegraph,* September 16, 2008, http://www.telegraph.co.uk/technology.

11. Andersen, *Reset* (New York: Random House, 2009).

12. Lev Grossman, "Time's Person of the Year: You," *Time,* December 13, 2006, http://www.time.com/time/magazine/article/0,9171,1569514,00. html.

13. Marshall Kirkpatrick, "Poll: US Attitudes about Internet Are Insane," *ReadWriteWeb,* October 25, 2007, http://www.readwriteweb.com/ archives/poll_us_attitudes_about_intern_1.php.

14. Catherine Smith, "Online Gaming Statistics Reveal How Much Time Gamers REALLY Spend Playing," *Huffington Post,* April 29, 2010, http:// www.huffingtonpost.com/2010/04/29/online-gaming-statistics_n_556879. html.

15. Funk, *Web 2.0 and Beyond* (Westport, CT: Praeger, 2009), xiii.

16. Kuhn, *The Structure of Scientific Revolutions,* 3rd ed. (Chicago: University of Chicago Press, 1996).

17. "What Americans Do Online: Social Media and Games Dominate Activity," *Nielsen Wire,* August 2, 2010, http://blog.nielsen.com/nielsen wire/online_mobile/what-americans-do-online-social-media-and-games-dominate-activity.

18. Austin Carr, "Facebook COO Sheryl Sandberg Is Embracing the End of Email, Here's Why," *Fast Company,* June 16, 2010, http://www. fastcompany.com/1660619/faccbook-coo-sheryl-sandberg-on-the-end-of-e-mail-branding-in-social-networks.

19. Kurzweil, "The Law of Accelerating Returns," *Kurzweil Accelerating Intelligence,* March 7, 2001, http://www.kurzweilai.net/the-law-of-accelerating-returns.

20. Ashlee Vance, "Merely Human? That's So Yesterday," *New York Times,* June 13, 2010, B1.

21. Bai, "The Shuffle President," *New York Times Magazine,* July 19, 2009, 11–12.

22. David Derbyshire, "Social Websites Harm Children's Brains: Chilling Warning to Parents from Top Neuroscientist," *Mail Online,* February 24, 2009, http://www.dailymail.co.uk/news/article-1153583/Social-web sites-harm-childrens-brains-Chilling-warning-parents-neuroscientist.html.

23. Carr, "Is Google Making Us Stupid? What the Internet Is Doing to Our Brains," *Atlantic,* July–August 2008, http://www.theatlantic.com/ magazine/print/2008/07/is-google-making-us-stupid/6868.

24. Lanier, *You Are Not a Gadget: A Manifesto* (New York: Alfred A. Knopf, 2010).

25. Quoted in Matt Richtel, "Digital Devices Deprive Brain of Needed Downtime," *New York Times,* August 25, 2010, B1.

26. Richtel, "Attached to Technology and Paying a Price," *New York Times,* June 7, 2010, A1.

27. Siegel, *Against the Machine* (New York: Spiegel & Grau, 2008), 152.

28. Manjoo, *True Enough* (New York: Wiley, 2008), 4, 17.

29. Hedges, review of *The Death and Life of American Journalism,* by Robert W. McChesney and John Nichols, Truthdig.com, February 25, 2010, http://www.truthdig.com/arts_culture/item/chris_hedges_on_the_death_and_life_of_american_journalism_20100226.

30. Sysomos, "Inside Blog Demographics," June 2010, http://www.sysomos.com/reports/bloggers.

31. Matt Sussman, "Blogging Revenues, Brands and Blogs, Technorati, "State of the Blogosphere 2009," http://technorati.com/blogging/feature/state-of-the-blogosphere-2009/

32. Sysomos, "Exploring the Use of Twitter around the World," January 14, 2010, http://www.sysomos.com/insidetwitter/geography

33. Amanda Lenhart and Susannah Fox, "Twitterpated: Mobile Americans Increasingly Take to Twitter," Pew Research Center, February 12, 2009, http://pewresearch.org/pubs/1117/twitter-tweet-users-demographics.

34. "Teens Don't Use Twitter, What the Tweet?" *Clean Cut Media,* August 7, 2009, http://www.cleancutmedia.com.

35. Mary Madden, "Older Adults and Social Media," Pew Internet and American Life Project, August 27, 2010, http://www.pewinternet.org/Reports/2010/Older-Adults-and-Social-Media.aspx.

36. "Better Access for Rural Areas to Modern Information and Communication Technologies," *Agricultural and Rural Development,* European Commission, March 3, 2009, http://ec.europa.eu/agriculture/rurdev/employment/ict/index_en.htm.

37. Edward Wyatt, "Broadband Availability to Expand," *New York Times,* June 28, 2010, B1.

38. Wyatt, "Broadband Availability."

39. Felix Contraras, "Young Latinos, Blacks Answer Call of Mobile Devices," NPR, December 1, 2009, http://www.npr.org/templates/story/story.php?Story ID=120852934.

40. Kristof, "The Daily Me," *New York Times,* March 19, 2009, A31.

41. Mark Landler and Brian Stelter, "Washington Taps into a Potent New Force in Diplomacy," *New York Times,* June 17, 2009, A12.

42. William Marshall, "The Wet Side of the Moon," *New York Times,* November 20, 2009, A35.

CHAPTER 2

1. Williams, *Culture and Society: 1780–1950* rev. ed. (New York: Columbia University Press, 1983), xvi.

2. Williams, *Culture and Society,* xvi.

3. Williams, *Culture and Society,* 327, 322.

4. Williams, *Keywords: A Vocabulary of Culture and Society* rev. ed. (New York: Oxford University Press, 1983), 195.

5. Robert Hughes, "Art: Upstairs and Downstairs at MOMA," *Time,* October 22, 1990, http://www.time.com/time/magazine/article/0,9171,971450,00.html.

6. Randy Kennedy, "Art That Needs No Hook or Pedestal," *New York Times,* March 28, 2010, WK2.

7. Hebdige, *Hiding in the Light* (New York: Routledge, 1989), 52.

8. Hebdige, *Hiding in the Light,* 55.

9. Quoted in Hebdige, *Hiding in the Light,* 73.

10. Hebdige, *Hiding in the Light,* 137.

11. Putnam, *Bowling Alone* (New York: Simon & Schuster, 2000), 372.

12. Putnam, *Bowling Alone,* 410.

13. Geertz, *The Interpretation of Cultures* (New York: Basic Books, 2000), 9, 11, 7.

14. Geertz, *Interpretation of Cultures,* 20.

15. Postman, *Technopoly: The Surrender of Culture to Technology* (New York: Vintage, 1993), 18.

16. Roger Bohn and James Short, "How Much Information?" University of California-San Diego Global Information Industry Center, January 2010, http://hmi.ucsd.edu/howmuchinfo_research_report_consum.php.

17. Postman, *Technopoly,* 60.

18. Miguel Helft, "Ballmer: The PC Will Continue to Thrive," *New York Times, Bits Blog,* June 3, 2010, http://bits.blogs.nytimes.com/2010/06/03/ballmer-the-pc-will-continue-to-thrivea.

19. G. Serrano, "5 Billion Cell Phone Users in 2010, UN Says," *Trends Updates,* February 19, 2010, http://trendsupdates.com/5-billion-cell-phone-users-in-2010-un-says/.

20. "The Revolution Has Gone Mobile," *New York Times,* February 20, 2010, A16.

21. Jenna Wortham, "Cellphones Now Used More for Data Than for Calls," *New York Times,* May 14, 2010, B1.

22. "More Cell Phone Users Use an App for That," Pew Research Center, July 10, 2010, http://pewresearch.org/pubs/1654/wireless-internet-users-cell-phone-mobile-data-applications.

23. World Internet Usage, 2010, *World Internet Statistics*, April 4, 2011, http://www.internetworldstats.com/stats.htm.

24. *BlogPulse,* April 2, 2011, http://www.blogpulse.com/.

25. Julia Boorstin, "Media Industry to Grow Faster Than US Economy," *Media Money,* August 10, 2010, http://www.cnbc.com/id/38645671.

26. Anderson, *The Long Tail* (New York: Hyperion, 2006).

27. Anderson, *The Long Tail,* 183–84.

28. Adam Singer, "49 Amazing Social Media, Web 2.0 and Internet Stats," *The Future Buzz,* January 2009, http://thefuturebuzz.com/2009/01/12/social-media-web-20-internet-numbers-stats/.

29. Quoted in Paul Stallard, "Digital PR Is like Word of Mouth on Steroids," April 6, 2010, http://paulstallard.wordpress.com/2010/04/06/digital-pr-is-like-word-of-mouth-on-steroids.

30. Biz Stone, *Who Let the Blogs Out?* (New York: St. Martin's Press, 2004), 192.

31. "State of the Blogosphere 2008," Technorati, http://technorati.com/blogging/feature/state-of-the-blogosphere-2008.

32. Aaron Smith, "New Numbers for Blogging and Blog Readership," Pew Internet and American Life Project, July 22, 2008, http://www.pewinternet.org/Commentary/2008/July/New-numbers-for-blogging-and-blog-readership.aspx.

33. Helen Leggatt, "Sysomos Reveals Blogger Demographics," *BizReport,* June 8, 2010, http://www.bizreport.com/2010/06/sysomos-reveals-blogger-demographics.html#.

34. Jason Lipshutz, "Lady Gaga to Steal Britney Spears' Twitter Crown," *Reuters US,* August 19, 2010, http://www.reuters.com/article/2010/08/19/us-gaga-idUSTRE67I69220100819America.

35. Barlow, *Blogging America: The New Public Sphere* (Westport, CT: Praeger, 2008), 20, 25, 1.

36. Sullivan, "Why I Blog," *Atlantic,* November 2008, http://www.theatlantic.com/magazine/archive/2008/11/why-i-blog/7060.

37. "State of the Blogosphere 2008."

38. Stan Schroeder, "Twitter Is Not Your Average Social Network," *Mashable,* August 2009, http://mashable.com/2009/06/02/twitter-users-dont-tweet/.

39. Lauren Dugan, "17 Things You Didn't Know about Twitter," Mediabistro.com, December 22, 2010, http://www.mediabistro.com/alltwitter/17-things-you-didnt-know-about-twitter_b350.

40. Turkle, *Life on the Screen* (New York: Simon & Schuster, 1995), 307.

41. Siegel, *Against the Machine,* 11.

42. Manjoo, *True Enough,* 176.

43. Manjoo, *True Enough,* 17.

44. Manjoo, *True Enough,* 53.

45. Anderson, *The Long Tail,* 63.

46. Wasik, *And Then There's This* (New York: Viking, 2009), 47.

47. Doug Gross, "Survey: More Americans Get Their News from Internet Than Newspapers and Radio," Pew Internet and American Life Project, March 1, 2010, http://www.pewinternet.org/Media-Mentions/2010/CNN-Tech-Online-News.aspx.

48. Palfrey and Gasser, *Born Digital* (New York: Basic Books, 2008), 62, 287.

49. Palfrey and Gasser, *Born Digital,* 266, 267–68.

50. President Barack Obama, commencement speech, Hampton University, Hampton, Virginia, May 9, 2010.

51. Palfrey and Gasser, *Born Digital,* 289.

CHAPTER 3

1. Siegel, *Against the Machine,* 160.

2. Penn, "America's Newest Profession: Bloggers for Hire," *Wall Street Journal,* April 21, 2009, http://online.wsj.com/article/SB124026415808636575.html.

3. Leggatt, "Sysomos Reveals Blogger Demographics."

4. "BlogPulse Stats," *BlogPulse,* August 31, 2010, http://www.blogpulse.com/.

5. Simon Clift, former marketing chief of Unilever, quoted in Paul Stallard, "Digital PR is like Word of Mouth on Steroids," *PaulStallard's TechnologyPR Agency Blog,* April 6, 2010, http://paulstallard.wordpress.com/2010/04/06/digital-pr-is-like-word-of-mouth-on-steroids/.

6. Jennifer Mendelsohn, "Honey, Don't Bother Mommy, I'm Too Busy Building My Brand," *New York Times,* March 14, 2010, ST1.

7. Pradnya Joshi, "When a Blogger Voices Approval, a Sponsor May Be Lurking," *New York Times,* July 17, 2010, B1.

8. BlogPulse, August 2010, http://www.blogpulse.com.

9. Dave White, "Day 2: The What and Why of Blogging," "State of the Blogosphere," *Technorati,* October 13, 2008, http://technorati.com/blogging/article/day-2-the-what-and-why/.

10. "New Media, Old Media: How Blogs and Social Media Agendas Relate and Differ from Traditional Press," Pew Research Center, May 23, 2010, http://www.pewresearch.org/pubs.1602/new-media-review-differences-from-tradtional-media.

11. Sysomos, "Inside Blog Demographics."

12. Amanda Lenhart, Kristen Purcell, Aaron Smith, and Kathryn Zickuhr, "Social Media and Young Adults," *Pew Internet and American Life*

Project, February 3, 2010, http://www.pewinternet.org/Reports/2010/So cial-Media-and-Young-Adults.aspx.

13. Sysomos, "Inside Blog Demographics."

14. Sysomos, "Inside Blog Demographics."

15. Alex Cheng and Mark Evans, "An In-Depth Look Inside the Twitter World," *Sysomos,* June 2009, http://www.sysomos.com/insidetwitter/.

16. "America's Newest Profession: Bloggers for Hire," *Wall Street Journal,* April 21, 2009, http://online.wsj.com/article/SB124026415808636575. html.

17. Dylan Stapleford, "*Gawker*'s No Longer a Blog," *The Wrap,* August 18, 2010, http://www.thewrap.com/media/column-post/gawker-media-redesign-20233.

18. Amanda Ernst, "*Huffington Post*'s Traffic More Than Doubles Year over Year," Mediabistro.com, January 19, 2010, http://www.mediabistro. com/fishbowlny/new_media/huffington_posts_traffic_more_than_dou bles_year_over_year_149222.asp.

19. Amanda Lenhart and Susannah Fox, "Bloggers," Pew Internet and American Life Project, July 19, 2006, http://www.pewinternet.org/ Reports/2006/Bloggers.aspx.

20. Aaron Smith, "Neighbors Online," Pew Internet and American Life Project, June 9, 2010, http://www.pewinternet.org/Reports/2010/Neigh bors-Online.aspx.

21. Brian Stelter, "From Treasury, an Invitation to Bloggers," *New York Times,* November 16, 2009, http://www.nytimes.com/2009/11/16/busi ness/media/16blog.htm.

22. Andy Sully, "Voices from the Middle," *Blue Collar Corner,* August 6, 2010, http://www.bluecollarcorner.com/blog/?p=750.

23. Barry Meier and Robert F. Worth, "Emirates to Cut Data Services of BlackBerry," *New York Times,* August 2, 2010, A1.

24. Bappa Majumdar and Devidutta Tripathy, "Blackberry Maker Wins Reprieve on India Shutdown," Yahoo! News, August 30, 2010, http://news. yahoo.com/s/nm/20100830/tc_nm/us_blackberry.

25. Noam Cohen, "Exploring News by the Amish Online," *New York Times,* September 21, 2009, B3.

26. "Technorati Top 100 Blogs," *Technorati,* April 2011, http://tech norati.com/blogs/top100.

27. "Best Blogs of 2010," *Time,* August 28, 2010, www.time.com/time/ specials/packages/completelist/0,29569, 1999770,00.html.

28. Dawn Olsen, "Arianna Huffington Interview: State of the Blogo-sphere 2009, *Technorati,* October 20, 2009, http://technorati.com/blog ging/article/arianna-huffington-interview-sotb-2009/.

29. Jenna Wortham, "Media Companies Try Getting Social with Tumblr," *New York Times,* August 2, 2010, B1.

30. Aaron Smith, "New Numbers for Blogging and Blog Readership," Pew Internet and American Life Project, July 22, 2008, http://www.pewinternet.org/Commentary/2008/July/New-numbers-for-blogging-and-blog readership.aspx; Lenhart et al., "Social Media and Young Adults," Pew Internet and American Life Project, February 3, 2010, http://www.pewinternet.org/Reports/2010/Social-Media-and-Young-Adults.aspx.

31. Elisa Camahort Page, "The BlogHer-iVillage 2010 Social Media Matters Study," BlogHer, http://www.blogher.com/files/Social_Media_Matters_2010.pdf.

32. Mercedes Bunz, "BBC Tells News Staff to Read Social Media," *PDA: the Digital Content Blog, Guardian,* February 10, 2010, http://www.guardian.co.uk/media/pda/2010/feb/10/bbc-news-social-media.

33. Alex Williams, "The Walter Winchells of Cyberspace," *New York Times,* April 1, 2010, E1.

34. Wasik, *And Then There's This,* 86–112.

35. Matt Sussman, "Blogging Revenues, Brands, and Blogs: State of the Blogosphere 2009, *Technorati,* http://technorati.com/blogging/article/day-4-blogging-revenues-brands-and/.

36. Noel Griese, "For the First Time Ever More POD Than Conventional Books," *Southern Review of Books,* June 16, 2009, http://www.southern reviewofbooks.blogspot.com/2009/06/for-the-first-time-ever-more-pod-than.html.

37. Jenna Wortham, "Public Provides Giggles; Bloggers Get the Book Deal," *New York Times,* April 18, 2009, B1.

38. Howard Kurtz, "*Washington Post* Writer David Weigel Resigns After Messages Leak," *Washington Post,* June 26, 2010, http://www.washintonpost.com/wp-dyn/content/article/2010/06/25/AR2010062504413.html.

39. Mark Leibovich, "Minutiae? In this White House, Call It News," *New York Times,* March 14, 2009, A10.

40. Stone, *Who Let the Blogs Out?* 12.

41. Scott Rosenberg, *Say Everything* (New York: Crown, 2009), 79.

42. Stone, *Who Let the Blogs Out?* 16–17, 20.

43. Rosenberg, *Say Everything,* 152.

44. Stone, *Who Let the Blogs Out?* 39–41.

45. Susannah Fox, "FCC: Broadband Adoption and Use in America," Pew Internet and American Life Project, February 23, 2010, http://www.pewinternet.org/Commentary/2010/February/FCC-Broadband-Adoption-and-Use-in-America.aspx.

46. Jon Sobel, "Day 1: Bloggers, Brands, and Consumers," "State of the Blogosphere 2010," *Technorati, November 2, 2010,* http://technorati.com/blogging/article/who-bloggers-brands-and-consumers-day/.

47. Palfrey and Gasser, *Born Digital,* 115.

48. John Horrigan, "Home Broadband Adoption 2009," Pew Internet & American Life Project, June 17, 2009, http://www.pewinternet.org/Reports/2009/10-Home-Broadband-Adoption-2009.aspx.

49. Turkle, *Life on the Screen,* 10.

50. Barlow, *Blogging America,* 5.

51. Douglas Quenqua, "Blogs Falling in an Empty Forest," *New York Times,* June 5, 2009, http://www.nytimes.com/2009/06/07/fashion/07blogs.html.

52. Keen, *The Cult of the Amateur* (New York: Crown, 2007). Quoted in Michiko Kakutani, "The Cult of the Amateur," the *New York Times,* June 29, 2007, http://www.nytimes.com/2007/06/29/books/29book.html.

CHAPTER 4

1. "Twitter, Facebook, Become Vital During Japanese Earthquake," *Huffington Post,* March 16, 2011, http://www.huffingtonpost.com/2011/03/11/twitter-facebook-become-v_n_834767.html (to copy editor: NO BYLINE on article).

2. "#numbers," *Twitter Blog,* March 14, 2011, http://blog.twitter.com/2011/03/numbers.html; Leena Rao, "Twitter Seeing 90 Million Tweets per Day, 25 Percent Contain Links," *TechCrunch,* September 14, 2010, http://techcrunch.com/2010/09/14/twitter-seeing-90-million-tweets-per-day/. Other Twitter demographics are compiled from the following websites: *Media Bistro,* February 22, 2010, http://www.mediabistro.com/baynewser/twitter/twitter_tops_50_million_tweets_per_day_152832.asp; *Quantcast,* August 13, 2010, http://www.quantcast.com/twitter.com; "The Twitter Clock: Real-Time Twitter Statistics," *Tweet Reports,* August 13, 2010, http://tweetreports.com/brand-monitoring/twitter-clock-twitter-brand-monitoring/; *Nick Burcher,* May 13, 2010, http://www.nickburcher.com/2010/05/twitter-facts-and-figures-latest.html.

3. Kevin Weil, "Measuring Tweets," *Twitter Blog,* February 22, 2010, http://blog.twitter.com/2010/02/measuring-tweets.html.

4. Aaron Smith and Lee Rainie, "8% of Online Americans Use Twitter," Pew Internet and American Life Project Report, December 9, 2010, http://www.pewinternet.org/Reports/2010/Twitter-Update-2010.aspx.

5. Grigoriadis, "America's Tweethearts," *Vanity Fair,* January 2010, http://www.vanityfair.com/culture/features/2010/02/twitter-201002.

6. "The Twitaholic.com Top 100 Twitterholics Based on Followers," *Twitaholic,* December 23, 2010, http://twitaholic.com/top100/followers/.

7. Alex Cheng and Mark Evans, "An In-Depth Look inside the Twitter World," Sysomos, August 2009, http://www.sysomos.com/insidetwitter/.

8. Cheng and Evans, "In-Depth Look."

9. "Tweaking the Twitter Home Page," *Twitter Blog,* March 30, 2010, www.blog.twitter.com.

10. Andre Yoskovich, "Ashton Kutcher is the King of Twitter," *After Dawn,* April 19, 2009, http://www.afterdawn.com/news/article. cfm/2009/04/19/ashton_kutcher_is_the_king_of_twitter.

11. Nick Burcher, "Twitter Facts and Figures, *Nick Burcher,* May 13, 2010, http://www.nickburcher.com/2010/05/twitter-facts-and-figures-latest.html.

12. Bill Heil and Mikolaj Piskorski, "New Twitter Research: Men Follow Men and Nobody Tweets," *Harvard Business Review,* June 1, 2009, http://blogs.hbr.org/cs/2009/06/new_twitter_research_men_follo.html.

13. "Twitter.com," *Quantcast,* May 2010, http://www.quantcast.com/ twitter.

14. Amanda Lenhart and Susannah Fox, "Twitter and Status Updating," Pew Internet and American Life Project, February 12, 2009, http://www. pewinternet.org/Reports/2009/Twitter-and-status-updating.aspx.

15. Twitter.com," *Quantcast,* May 2010, http://www.quantcast.com/ twitter.com.

16. Quoted in Steven Levy, "Mob Rule! How Users Took Over Twitter," *Wired,* October 19, 2009, http://www.wired.com/magazine/2009/10ff_twit ter/all/1.

17. Quoted in Ed Oswald, "Study: No One Will Pay for Twitter," *Technologizer,* July 27, 2010, http://www.technologizer.com/2010/07/27/study-no-one-will-pay-for-twitter.

18. David Sarno, "Twitter Creator Jack Dorsey Illuminates the Site's Founding Document, Part I," *L.A. Times Technology,* February 18, 2009, http://latimesblogs.latimes.com/technology/2009/02/twitter-creator.html.

19. "What's Happening?" *Twitter Blog,* November 19, 2009, http:// www.blog.twitter.com.

20. Sarno, "Twitter Creator," February 18, 2009.

21. Ibid.

22. Charles Arthur, "How Twitter and Flicker Recorded the Mumbai Attacks," *Guardian,* November 27, 2008, http://www.guardian.co.uk/ technology/2008/nov/27/mubai-terror-attacks-twitter-.

23. Brian Stelter and Noam Cohen, "Citizen Journalists Provided Glimpses of Mumbai Attacks," *New York Times,* November 30, 2008, A26.

24. Horrocks, "BBC Tells News Staff."

25. "Zogby Interactive: 49% of U.S. Adults Trust Microsoft, Google, & Apple," *IBPOE Zogby International,* June 17, 2010, http://www.zogby.com/news/ReadNews.cfm?ID=1871.

26. "What's Happening?" *Twitter Blog,* November 19, 2009, http://www.blog.twitter.com/2009/11/whats-happening.html.

27. "The Twitter Rules and Best Practices," http://support.twitter.com/groups/31-twitter-basics/topics/114-guidelines-best-practices/articles/69214-rules-and-best-practices. Twitter Support is at http://blog.twitter.com/search?q=Twitter+support.

28. McLuhan, "Prologue," in *The Gutenberg Galaxy: The Making of Typographic Man* (Toronto: University of Toronto Press, 1962), 1.

29. McLuhan, *Gutenberg Galaxy,* 20, 24.

30. Guy Trebay, "Places, Everyone! Take the Usual Places," *New York Times,* February 18, 2010, E8.

31. Carr, "Why Twitter Will Endure," *New York Times,* January 3, 2010, http://www.nytimes.com/2010/01/03/weekinreview/03carr.html.

32. Clive Thompson, "Clive Thompson on the New Literacy," *allthingsd.com,* August 31, 2009, http://voices.allthingsd.com/20090831/clive-thompson-on-the-new-literacy/.

33. Orenstein, "I Tweet, Therefore I Am," *New York Times,* August 1, 2010, MM11.

34. Sara Konrath, "The Empathy Gap," *Psychology Today,* June 20, 2010, http://www.psychologytoday.com/blog/the-empathy-gap/201006/the-end-empathy.

35. Tim Collins, *The Little Book of Twitter,* quoted in Matthew Moore, "Twitter: Great Works of Literature Shortened into Tweets," *The Telegraph,* May 11, 2009, http://www.telegraph.co.uk/technology/twitter/5309001/Twitter-Great-works-of-literature-shortened-into=tweets.html.

36. Halpern, *Sh*t My Dad Says* (New York: It Books/Harper-Collins, 2010).

37. Thom Geier, "'Ice Storm' Author Tweets a Short Story," *ew.com,* November 24, 2009, http://shelf-life.ew.com/2009/11/24/rick-moody-twitter-story/.

38. "Pulse of the Nation," College of Computer and Information Science, Northeastern University and Harvard University, September 2009, http://www.ccs.neu.edu/home/amislove/twittermood/.

39. "Why Do People Use Twitter?" *Social Media Optimization,* August 17, 2009, http://social-media-optimization.com/2009/08/why-do-people-use-twitter/.

40. Ryan Kelly, "Twitter Study Yields Interesting Results about Usage—40% Is 'Pointless Babble,'" Pear Analytics, August 12, 2009, http://www.pearanalytics.com/blog/2009/twitter-study-reveals-interesting-results-40-percent-pointless-babble/.

41. "Pop Quiz Communications; Networking," *New York Times,* July 25, 2010, *Education Life,* ED31.

42. Michael Schwirtz, "Bluster on Twitter, and Off It Too, from Russia's NATO Envoy," *New York Times,* February 13, 2010, A4.

43. Tonia Reis, "Why People Use Twitter, Facebook, MySpace, and MyYearbook, *The Realtime Report,* June 24, 2010, http://therealtimereport.com/page/38/?redirected_from=twtrcon.com.

44. Ryan Kelly, "Twitter Study Yields Interesting Results about Usage—40% Is 'Pointless Babble,'" *Pear Analytics,* August 12, 2009, http://www.pearanalytics.com/blog/2009/twitter-study-reveals-interesting-results-40-percent-pointless-babble/.

45. Anderson, *Dooce.com,* July 26, 2010, http://www.dooce.com.

46. David Carr, "Why Twitter Will Endure."

47. Packer, "Stop the World," *New Yorker,* January 29, 2010, http://www.newyorker.com/online/blogs/georgepacker/2010/01/stop-the-world.html.

CHAPTER 5

1. Rich, "The American Press on Suicide Watch," *New York Times,* May 10, 2009, WK8.

2. Hendrick Hertzberg, "Open Secrets," *New Yorker,* August 2, 2010, 17.

3. Hirschorn, "End Times," *Atlantic,* January–February 2009, http://www.theatlantic.com/magazine/archive/2009/01/end-times/7220/.

4. Jeremy W. Peters, "Some Newsrooms Shift Coverage Based on What Is Popular Online," *New York Times,* September 6, 2010, B1.

5. David Simon, "Old and New Media Go to Washington," *On the Media,* May 8, 2009, http://www.onthemedia.org/transcripts/2009/05/08/01.

6. Keller, "Henry Luce, Editor in Chief," *New York Times Book Review,* April 25, 2010, BR1.

7. Huffington, keynote speech at American Association of Advertising Agencies, March 1, 2010, http://blog.artsusa.org/2010/06/27/arianna-huffington-keynote.

8. Hedges, review of *Death and Life of American Journalism.*

9. Robert W. McChesney and John Nichols, *The Death and Life of American Journalism* (Philadelphia: First Nation Books, 2010), 27.

10. McChesney and Nichols, *Death and Life,* 11, 32.

11. "Most Online News Readers Use 5 Sites or Fewer, Study Says," *New York Times,* March 15, 2010, B2.

12. McChesney and Nichols, *Death and Life,* 33–35.

13. "For the First Time, More People get News Online than from Newspapers," *Mashable.com,* March 2011, http://mashable.com/2011/03/15/online-versus-newspaper-news/.

14. "The State of the News Media 2010," http://pewresearch.org/pubs/1523/state-of-the-news-media-2010.

15. "2010 Digital Future Report," Center for the Digital Future at the University of Southern California Annenberg School for Communication and Journalism, July 23, 2010, http://www.digitalcenter.org/pages/current_report.asp?intGlobalId=19.

16. Tim Arango, "Fall in Newspaper Sales Accelerates to Pass 7%," *New York Times,* April 28, 2010, B3.

17. "State of the News Media 2010."

18. Lymari Morales, "In U.S., Confidence in Newspapers, TV News Remains a Rarity," Gallup, August 13, 2010, http://www.gallup.com/poll/142133/Confidence-Newspapers-News-Remains-Rarity.aspx.

19. Rosenberg, *Say Everything,* 83.

20. Rosenberg, *Say Everything,* 85.

21. Huffington, keynote speech at American Association of Advertising Agencies.

22. In February 2011, AOL bought the *Huffington Post* in a $315 million deal that positions Huffington as president and editor-in-chief of the newly-created Huffington Post Media Group. Jeremy W. Peters and Verne G. Kopytoff, "Betting on News, AOL Buys Huffington Post," *New York Times,* February 7, 2011, http://www.nytimes.com/2011/02/07/business/media/07aol.html.

23. Eric Boehlert, *Bloggers on the Bus* (New York: Free Press, 2009), 171–77.

24. Lionel Beehner, "Social Networking Butterfly," *New York Times,* July 15, 2010, E7.

25. Javier C. Hernandez, "Vote Endorses Muslim Center near Ground Zero," *New York Times,* May 26, 2010, A23.

26. "The Building of the Islamic Mosque in NYC has Finally Gotten Approval!" *White Noise Insanity,* August 4, 2010, http://www.whitenoi

seinsanity.com/2010/08/04/the-building-of-the-Islamic-mosque-in-nyc-has-finally-gotten-approval/comment-page-1.

27. Gail Shister, "The Shot Heard 'round the Industry, Backpack Journalism on the Rise," Mediabistro.com, February 26, 2010, http://www.media bistro.com/tvnewser/abc/changes_come_to_network_news153227.aspx.

28. "Most Online News Readers."

29. Tina Brown, interview with Mary Cross, December 9, 2009.

30. McChesney and Nichols, *Death and Life,* 73.

31. Rosenberg, *Say Everything,* 152.

32. Rosenberg, *Say Everything,* 146.

33. Rosenberg, *Say Everything,* 153.

34. Boehlert, *Bloggers on the Bus,* 123.

35. David Carr, "Journalists, Provocateurs, Maybe Both," *New York Times,* July 26, 2010, B1.

36. Rosenberg, *Say Everything,* 343.

37. Quoted in Rosenberg, *Say Everything,* 343.

38. Sridhar Pappu, "Washington's New Brat Pack Masters Media," *New York Times,* March 27, 2011, ST1.

39. "New Media Review Differences from Traditional Press," Pew Research Center, August 19, 2010, http://pewresearch.org/pubs/1602/new-media-review-differences-from-traditional-press.

40. Jeremy W. Peters, "At Yahoo, Using Searches to Steer News Coverage," *New York Times,* July 5, 2010, B1.

41. Brooks, "The Culture of Exposure," *New York Times,* June 25, 2010, A31.

42. Anderson, *Long Tail,* 186.

43. Dennis Overbye, "Rumors in Astrophysics Spread at Light Speed," *New York Times,* August 3, 2010, D1.

44. Choe Sang-Hun, "North Korea Takes to Twitter and YouTube, *New York Times,* August 17, 1010, A7.

45. Manjoo, *True Enough,* 192.

46. Boehlert, *Bloggers on the Bus,* 169.

47. Boehlert, *Bloggers on the Bus,* 171–77.

48. Bunz, "BBC Tells News Staff."

CHAPTER 6

1. Naomi S. Baron, *Always On* (New York: Oxford University Press, 2008), 169, 171.

2. Pritchard, "The Readers' Editor . . . the Four-Letter Word Conundrum," *Guardian Observer,* August 22, 2010, http://www.guardian.co.uk/theobserver/2010/aug/22/readers-editor-swear-words-ricky-gervais.

3. Barlow, *Blogging America,* 56.

4. Monck, "Can Apps Save News Journalism?" *Guardian Comment,* August 23, 2010, http://www.guardian.co.uk/commentisfree/2010/aug/23/can-apps-save-news-journalism.

5. Chen, "North Korean has only 65 Friends on Facebook and Is Gay," *Gawker Valleywag,* August 20, 2010, http://gawker.com/5617946/north-korea-has-only-65-friends-on-facebook-and-is-gay.

6. Stableford, "How to Write Like *Gawker,*" *Folio,* February 15, 2008, http://www.foliomag.com/2008/how-write-gawker.

7. Armstrong, "Wherein I Return to My Roots," *Dooce.com,* July 12, 2010, http://www.dooce.com/2010/07/12/wherein-i-return-my-roots.

8. Armstrong, "The Night of the Missing Dogs," *Dooce.com,* August 19, 2010, http://www.dooce.com/2010/08/19/night-missing-dogs.

9. Gregg Kilday and Kim Masters, "Jennifer Anniston Stuck in Second Tier with new Flop," *Hollywood Reporter,* August 24, 2010, http://www.hollywoodreporter.com/hr/content_display/film/news/e31a4556ea7eb5985d2c8ab9508f467776.

10. Chris Barr and Senior Editors at Yahoo! *The Yahoo! Style Guide.* (New York: St. Martin's Press, 2010), 3–16.

11. Baron, *Always On,* 171.

12. Douglas Quenqua, "Dude You Are So (Not) Obama," *New York Times,* August 23, 2009, ST1.

13. Anand Girdharadas, "Follow My Logic? A Connective Word Takes the Lead," *New York Times,* May 30, 2010, WK3.

14. Tannen, *You Just Don't Understand: Men and Women in Conversation* (New York: Ballantine, 1990).

15. Baron, *Always On,* 50.

16. Herring, ed., *Computer-Mediated Communication: Linguistic, Social, and Cross-Cultural Perspectives* (Amsterdam: John Benjamins, 1996).

17. Herring, "Gender and Power in Online Communication," in *The Handbook of Language and Gender,* ed. J. Holmes and M. Meyerhoff (Oxford: Blackwell, 2003), http://scholarworks.iu.edu/dspace/bitstream/handle/2022/1024/WP01–05B/html.

18. Herring, "Gender and Power."

19. Wallace, *The Psychology of the Internet* (Cambridge: Cambridge University Press, 1999), 220.

20. Steve Lohr, "Study Measures the Chatter of the News Cycle," *New York Times,* July 13, 2009, B1.

21. Quoted in Menand, "Thumbspeak: Is Texting Here to Stay?" *New Yorker,* October 20, 2008, 86–87, http://www.newyorker.com/arts/critics/books/2008/10/20/081020crbo_books_menand.

22. Menand, "Thumbspeak," 86.

23. Menand, "Thumbspeak," 86.

24. Robin "Roblimo" Miller, "Clay Shirky Explains Internet Evolution," *Slashdot,* March 13, 2001, http://tech.slashdot.org/article.pl?sid=01/03/13/1420210&mode=nocomment.

25. John Metcalfe, "On the Twitter Patrol," *New York Times,* April 29, 2010, E8.

26. Quoted in Robert Feder, "Memo Puts WGN News Staffers at a Loss for Words," March 10, 2010, http://www.blogs.vocalo.org/feder/2010/03/memo-puts-WGN-news-staffers-at-a-loss-for-words-17374.

27. *Language Log,* http://www.languagelog.1dc.uppenn.edu.

28. Quoted in Cynthia Haven, "The New Literacy: Stanford Study Finds Richness and Complexity in Students' Writing," *Stanford News,* October 12, 2009, http://news.stanford.edu/news/2009/october12/lunsford-writing-research-101209.html.

29. Haven, "New Literacy."

30. Sam Dillon, "Stagnant National Reading Scores Lag behind Math," *New York Times,* March 25, 2010, A18.

31. Teddy Wayne, "Falling Sales for the Printed Word," *New York Times,* April 19, 2010, B2.

32. Tamar Lewin, "If Your Kids Are Awake, They're Probably Online," *New York Times,* January 20, 2010, A1.

33. Carr, "Is Google Making Us Stupid?"

34. Carr, "Is Google Making Us Stupid?"

35. Wolf, *Proust and the Squid: The Story and Science of the Reading Brain* (New York: Harper, 2007).

36. Carr, "Is Google Making Us Stupid?"

37. Johnson, *Everything Bad Is Good for You* (New York: Riverhead, 2005).

38. Cascio, "Get Smarter," *Atlantic,* July–August 2009, http://www.theatlantic.com/magazine/archive/2009/07/get-smarter/7548/.

39. Claire Cain Miller, "E-Books Top Hardcovers at Amazon," *New York Times,* July 20, 2010, B1.

40. Norimitsu Onishi, "Thumbs Race as Japan's Best Sellers Go Cellular," *New York Times,* January 20, 2008, A1.

41. David W. Martin, "Apple Reveals New Service for Authors to Sell Their Books Directly in the Bookstore," *MacLife,* May 26, 2010, http://www.maclife.com/article/news/apple_reveals_new_service_authors_sell_their_ books_directly-ibookstore.

42. Quoted in Nick Bilton, "Roll-Up Computers and Their Kin," *New York Times,* June 27, 2010, WK3.

43. Quoted in Bilton, "Roll-Up Computers."

44. Quoted in Frederic Lardinois, "What the Internet Will Look Like in 2020," *ReadWriteWeb,* February 19, 2010, http://www.readwriteweb.com/archives/what_will_the_internet_look_like_in_2020_heres_wha.php.

45. Nicholas Kulish, "It's 'Mixing,' Not Plagiarism," *New York Times,* February 12, 2010, A4.

46. Abhi, "How Kaavya Viswanathan Got Rich, Got Caught, and Got Ruined," *Sepia Mutiny,* April 24, 2006, http://www.sepiamutiny.com/sepia/archives/003294.html.

47. Trip Gabriel, "Plagiarism Lines Blur for Students in a Digital Age," *New York Times,* August 2, 2010, A1.

48. Quoted in Gabriel, "Plagiarism Lines Blur."

49. Quoted in Gabriel, "Plagiarism Lines Blur."

50. Lera Boroditsky, "Lost in Translation," *Wall Street Journal,* July 24, 2010, http://online.wsj.com/NA_WSJ_PUB:SB10001424052748703467 304575383131592767868.html.

CHAPTER 7

1. Jim Dwyer, "Four Nerds and a Cry to Arms against Facebook," *New York Times,* May 12, 2010, A19.

2. Stephanie Clifford, "Consumer Groups Say Proposed Privacy Bill Is Flawed," *New York Times,* May 5, 2010, B3.

3. Polly Sprenger, "Sun on Privacy: 'Get Over it,'" *Wired,* January 1999, http://www.wired.com/politics.law/news/1999/01/17536.

4. Nicholas Carr, *The Big Switch: Rewiring the World, from Edison to Google* (New York: W. W. Norton, 2009), 190.

5. Mike Masnick, "Will Kids Change Their Names as They Become Adults to Hide from Their Google Permanent Record?" *Techdirt,* August 18, 2010, http://www.techdirt.com/articles/201000816/122112106.html.

6. Casey, "Replay It: Google Search across the Twitter Archive," *Official Google Blog,* April 14, 2010, http://www.googleblog.blogspot.com/2010/04/replay-it-google-search-across-twitter.html.

7. Hibah Yousuf, "Google and Library of Congress Archive Tweets," *CNN Money,* April 14, 2010, http://money.cnn.com/2010/04/14/technol ogy/Google_Twitter_archive/index.htm.

8. Nick Bilton, "Price of Facebook Privacy? Start Clicking," *New York Times,* May 13, 2010, B8.

9. Jenna Wortham, "Facebook Glitch Brings New Privacy Worries," *New York Times,* May 6, 2010, C1.

10. Jenna Wortham. "New Facebook Location Sparks Privacy Concerns," *New York Times,* August 18, 2010, http://www.nytimes.com/2010/08/18/ new-face-book-location-sparks-privacy-concerns.

11. Claire Cain Miller, "Twitter Will Add Places to Twitter Posts," *New York Times, Bits Blog,* June 14, 2010, http://www.bits.blogs.nytimes. com/2010/06/14/twitter-will-add-places-to-twitter-posts.

12. Sakthi Prasad and Lincoln Feast, "Amazon Files Lawsuit to Block North Carolina's Request," Reuters, April 20, 2010, http://www.reuters. com/article/idUSTRE63JOLFE20100420.

13. Dwyer, "Four Nerds."

14. Mike Melanson, "Facebook: As Unpopular as Airlines, Cable Companies, and the IRS," *ReadWriteWeb,* July 20, 2010, http://www.readwrite web.com/archives/facebook-as-unpopular-as-airlines-cable-companies. php.

15. Mark Alvarez, "Study: Teens Just as Concerned with Online Privacy as Adults," *L'Atelier,* http://www.atelier-us.com/internet-usage/article/ study-teens-just-as-concerned-with-online-privacy-as-adults.

16. Mary Madden and Aaron Smith, "Reputation Management and Social Media," Pew Internet and American Life Project, May 2010, http:// www.pewinternet.org/Reports/2010/Reputation-Management.aspx.

17. Electronic Privacy Information Center, "Spotlight on Surveillance," http://www.epic.org/privacy/surveillance/spotlight/0505.

18. Julia Angwin, "The Web's New Gold Mine: Your Secrets," *Wall Street Journal,* July 30, 2010, http://online.wsj.com/article/SB1000/42405 2748703940904575395077351298940404.html.

19. Angwin, "Web's New Gold Mine."

20. Emma Barnett, "Google Street View: Survey Raises Privacy Concerns," *The Telegraph,* March 12, 2010, http://www.telegraph.co.uk/ technology/google/7430245/Google-Street-View-survey-raises-privacy-concerns.html.

21. Tamar Lewin, "Teenage Insults, Scrawled on Web, Not on Wall," *New York Times,* May 6, 2010, A1.

22. Simon Wiesenthal Center, "Online Hate Sites Grow."

23. Amanda Lenhart, "Cyberbullying 2010: What the Research Tells Us," *Slideshare.net,* http://www.pewinternet.org/Presentations/2010/May/Cyberbullying-2010.aspx.

24. Sameer Hinduja and Justin W. Patchin, "Summary of Our Cyberbullying Research from 2004–2010," Cyberbullying Research Center, February 2010, http://www.cyberbullying.us/research.php.

25. Ibid.

26. Salynn Boyles, "What Motivates Kids Who Are Bullies?" WebMD, March 25, 2010, http://www.webmd.com/parenting/news/20100325/what-motivates-kids-who-are-bullies.

27. Richard A. Falkenrath, "Texting with Terrorists," *New York Times,* August 10, 2010, A25.

28. Lucie Morillon, "Web 2.0 versus Control 2.0,"*Business Insider,* March 12, 2010, http://www.businessinsider.com/web-20-versus-control-20-lucie-morillonreporters-without-borders-2010-3.

29. Quoted in Charles Arthur, "Google Releases Tool to Show Government Censorship Requests," *Guardian,* April 20, 2010, http://www.guardian.co.uk/technology2010/apr/20/google-google-street-view.

30. Juliana Gruenwald, "New Google Tool Highlights Data Removal Requests," *National Journal,* April 20, 2010, http://techdailydose.national-journal.com/2010/04/new-google-tool-highlights-dat.php.

31. David Barboza and Miguel Helft, "China Renews Google's License," *New York Times,* July 10, 2010, B1.

32. Jonathan Ansfield, "China Tests New Controls on Twitter-Style Services," *New York Times,* July 17, 2010, A7.

33. "Frequently Asked Questions about Copyright," *Chilling Effects*, http://www.chillingeffects.org/copyright/faq.cgi#QID447

34. "The Digital Millennium Copyright Act," University of California-Los Angeles Online Institute for Cyberspace Law and Policy, http://gseis.ucla.edu/iclp/dmcal.html.

35. Eileen Alt Powell and Howard Angione, eds., *The Associated Press Stylebook and Libel Manual* (New York: Associated Press, 1980).

36. *The Associated Press Stylebook and Libel Manual,* pp. 251–52.

37. Wendy Davis, "Judge Rules News Station Is Immune from 'Cyber Libel' Resulting from Commenters," *Media Post,* September 1, 2010, http://www.mediapost.com/publications/?fa=Articles.showArticle&art_aid=134815.

38. Media Law Resource Center, "MLRC: Actions Against Online Speech," April 12, 2009, http://mlrcblogsuits.blogspot.com/2009_04_12_archive.html.

39. Peter Lattman, "Mark Cuban to Face S.E.C. Insider Case Again," *Dealbook, New York Times,* September 21, 2010, http://dealbook.nytimes.com/2010/09/21/court-reinstates-s-e-c-case-against-mark-cuban/.

40. Chloe Albanesius, "Report: Courtney Love Settles Twitter Defamation Suit for $430K" *Yahoo! News,* March 4, 2011, http://news.yahoo.com/s/ap/20110304/ap_on_en_mu/us_courtney_love_twitter_suit.

41. Siobhain Butterworth, "Can live-blogs and Twitter take court reporting into the 21st century?," *Afua Hirsch's Law Blog, Guardian,* July 28, 2010, http://www.guardian.co.uk/law/afua-hirsch-law-blog/2010/jul/28/live-blogging-tweeting-court-reporting.

42. Mark Milian, "Twitter Trouble: Mark Cuban Fined, Courtney Love Sued—over Tweets," *L.A. Times Technology Blog,* March 30, 2009, http://www.latimesblogs.latimes.com/technology/2009/03/markcuban/twitter.html.

43. Quoted in Miguel Helft, "Firm Settles over Faking App Reviews on iTunes," *New York Times,* August 27, 2010, C1.

44. Dan Frosch, "Venting Online, Consumers Can Find Themselves in Court," *New York Times,* June 1, 2010, A1.

45. Manjoo, *True Enough,* 4, 17–18, 53.

46. Manjoo, *True Enough,* 17–18, 150.

47. Manjoo, *True Enough,* 81.

48. Twitter, "Parody, Commentary, and Fan Accounts Policy," Twitter Terms of Service, 2011, http://www.twitter.zendesk.com/entries/106373-parody-commentary-and-fan-accounts-policy.

49. Riva Richmond, "Stolen Facebook Accounts for Sale," *New York Times,* May 3, 2010, B3.

50. Claire Cain Miller and Brian Stelter, "Web Plan Is Dividing Companies," *New York Times,* August 12, 2010, B1.

51. Edward Wyatt, "Google and Verizon Near Deal on Web Pay Tiers," *New York Times,* August 5, 2010, A1.

CHAPTER 8

1. Prensky, "Digital Natives, Digital Immigrants," October 2001, htttp://www.marcprensky.com/writing/Prensky%20-%20Digital%20Natives,%20Digital%20Immigrants%20-%20Part1.pdf.

2. Palfrey and Gasser, *Born Digital,* 62.

3. Prensky, "Digital Natives."

4. Wolf, *Proust and the Squid,* 217.

5. Wolf, *Proust and the Squid,* 215.

6. Prensky, "Digital Natives."

7. comScore, "Twitter Demographics," *Marketing Charts,* February 2010,http://www.marketingcharts.com/interactive/facebook-twitter-grow-more-than-100–11943/comscore-twitter-demographic-segment-trend-feb-2010jpg/.

8. Elsa Camahort Page, "The BlogHer—iVillage 2010 Social Media Matters Study," BlogHer, http://www.blogher.com/files/Social_Media_Matters_2010.pdf.

9. Quantcast, "Twitter Demographics," 2010, http://www.quantcast.com/twitter.com.

10. Tara Parker-Pope, "Is Every Generation Self-Absorbed?" *Well: Tara Parker-Pope on Health,* August 2, 2010, http://well.blogs.nytimes.com/2010/08/02/is-every-generation-self-absorbed/.

11. Twenge, "Is There an Epidemic of Narcissism Today?," *Psychology Today,* May 8, 2009, http://www.psychologytoday.com/blog/the-narcissism-epidemic/200905/is-there-epidemic-narcissism-today.

12. Robin Marantz Henig, "What Is It about 20-Somethings?" *New York Times,* August 22, 2010, MM28.

13. Henig, "What Is It about 20-Somethings?"

14. Quoted in Teddy Wayne, "Managing Reputations on Social Sites," *New York Times,* June 17, 2010, B2.

15. Quoted in "Empathy: College Students Don't Have as Much as They Used to, Study Says," *ScienceDaily,* May 29, 2010, http://www.sciencedaily.com/releases/2010/05/100528081434.htm.

16. Beloit College, "Mindset List," August 2010, http://www.beloit.edu/mindset/2014.php.

17. Roiphe, "The Language of Fakebook," *New York Times,* August 15, 2010, "Sunday Styles," 2.

18. Goffman, *The Presentation of Self in Everyday Life* (New York: Anchor, 1959), 22.

19. Robert Ezra Park, *Race and Culture* (Glencoe, IL: Free Press, 1950), 249.

20. Sorgatz, "The Microfame Game," *New York Magazine,* June 17, 2008, http://nymag.com/news/media/47958.

21. Lasch, *The Culture of Narcissism,* rev. ed. (New York: W. W. Norton, 1991), 14, 50, 10.

22. Keith Hampton, Lauren Sessions, Eu Ja Her, and Lee Rainie, "Social Isolation and New Technology," Pew Internet and American Life Project,

November 4, 2009, http://www.pewinternet.org/Reports/2009/18—Social-Isolation-and-New-Technology.aspx.

23. Nicki Dowling, "An Ugly Toll of Technology: Impatience and Forgetfulness," *New York Times,* June 7, 2010, A13.

24. Parker-Pope, "Is Every Generation Self-Absorbed?"

25. Choe Sang-Hun, "South Korea Expands Aid for Internet Addiction," *New York Times,* May 28, 2010, A4.

26. Hampton et al., "Social Isolation and New Technology."

27. Aaron Smith, "Neighbors Online," Pew Internet and American Life Project, June 9, 2010, http://www.pewinternet.org/Reports/2010/Neighbors-Online.aspx.

28. Clair Bates, "How Michael Jackson's Death Shut Down Twitter, Brought Chaos to Google . . . and 'Killed Off' Jeff Goldblum," *Mail Online,* June 26, 2009, http://www.dailymail.co.uk/sciencetech/article-1195651/How-Michael-Jacksons-death-shut-Twitter-overwhelmed-Google–killed-Jeff-Goldblum.htm

29. Ryan Kelly, "Twitter Study Reveals Interesting Results."

30. Katelyn Sabochik, "Education Means Emancipation," *The White House Blog,* May 10, 2010, http://www.whitehouse.gov/blog/2010/05/10/education-means-emancipation.

31. Asylum Staff, "The Internet Will Fail—Bold Predictions That Completely Bombed," *Asylum For All Mankind,* April 21, 2010, http://www.asylum.com/2010/04/21/internet-will-fail-bold-predictions-that-bombed/.

32. Keen, *Cult of the Amateur,* 3, 204, 68, 205.

33. Siegel, *Against the Machine,* 4, 3, 134, 7.

34. Siegel, *Against the Machine,* 88, 6, 19, 89.

35. Siegel, *Against the Machine,* 89.

36. Siegel, *Against the Machine,* 98.

37. Lanier, *You Are Not a Gadget,* 4, 15, 5–6.

38. Roger Bohn, "How Much Information?" Global Information Industry Center, University of California-San Diego, January 2010, http://hmi.ucsd.edu/howmuchinfo_research_report_consum.php.

39. Janna Anderson and Lee Rainie, "Future of the Internet IV," Pew Internet and American Life Project, February 19, 2010, http://pewinternet.org/Reports/2010/Future-of-the-Internet-IV.aspx.

40. Bohn, "How Much Information?"

41. Richard Perez-Pena, "New Sites Rethink Anonymous Online Comments," *New York Times,* April 12, 2010, B1.

42. Palfrey and Gasser, *Born Digital,* 85–86.

43. Rosenberg, "Online Comments Need Moderation, Not 'Real' Names," *Slate*, April 13, 2010, http://bx.businessweek.com/online-real-estate/view? url=http%3A%2F%2Fwww.salon.com%2Fnews%2Ffeature%2F201 0%2F04%2F13%2Fnewspaper_online_comments_moderation_open 2010%2Findex.html.

44. Quantcast, "Formspring.com," July 31, 2010, http://www.quantcast. com/formspring.com.

45. Frosch, "Venting Online."

46. Chris Anderson and Michael Wolff, "The Web Is Dead, Long Live the Internet," *Wired,* August 17, 2010, http://www.wired.com/ magazine/2010/08/ff_webrip/all/1.

CHAPTER 9

1. Steve Lohr, "The Future of Broadband—in Tasmania," *New York Times, Bits Blog,* August 4, 2010, http://bits.blogs.nytimes.com/2010/08/04/ the-future-of-broadband-in-tasmania/.

2. Haraway, "A Cyborg Manifesto: Science, Technology, and Social-ist-Feminism in the Late Twentieth Century," in *Simians, Cyborgs, and Women: The Reinvention of Nature* (New York: Routledge, 1991).

3. "Usage and Population Statistics," *Internet World Statistics*, March 31, 2011, http://www.internetworldstats.com/stats.html.

4. Wasik, *And Then There's This,* 28.

5. Clive Thompson, "Brave New World of Digital Intimacy," *New York Times Sunday Magazine,* September 7, 2008, MM42.

6. Kakutani, "Texts without Context," *New York Times,* March 21, 2010, AR1.

7. Lanier, *You Are Not a Gadget,* 182.

8. Rubel, "It's Time to Prepare for the End of the Web as We Know It," *Ad Age Digital,* July 12, 2010, http://www.adage.com/digital/ article?article_id=144867.

9. Anderson and Wolff, "The Web Is Dead."

10. Sorgatz, "Microfame Game"; and Beehner, "Social Networking Butterfly."

11. Negroponte, *Being Digital,* 14.

12. Negroponte, *Being Digital,* 4.

13. Quoted in Catone, "Last 5 Years in Blogging."

14. Christina Warren, "Google TV Set for Fall Launch," *Mashable,* September 8, 2010, http://mashable.com/2010/09/07/google-tv-launch/.

15. "A Virtual Counter-Revolution," *Economist,* September 2, 2010, http://www.economist.com/research/articlesBySubject/displaystory.cfm?subjectid=348963&story_id=16941635.

16. Laura Rich, "Tapping the Wisdom of the Crowd," *New York Times,* August 5, 2010, B8.

17. Marshall Kirkpatrick, "Google's Eric Schmidt on What the Web Will Look Like in 5 Years," *ReadWriteWeb,* October 27, 2009, http://www.readwriteweb.com/archives/google_web_in_five_years.php.

18. Richard McManus, "Eric Schmidt Defines Web 3.0," *ReadWriteWeb,* August 7, 2010, http://www.readwriteweb.com/archives/eric_schmidt_defines_web_30.php.

19. John Markoff, "Computers as Invisible as the Air," *New York Times,* September 5, 2010, WK2.

20. Rebecca Jeschke, "Reading, Writing, and RFID Chips: A Scary Back-to-School Future in California," Electronic Frontier Foundation (EFF), August 30, 2010, http://www.eff.org/deeplinks/2010/08/reading-writing-and-rfid-chips-scary-back-school.

21. Michael Wines, "China Will Require ID for Cellphone Numbers; Noncompliance Means No Service," *New York Times,* September 2, 2010, A14.

22. Mark Penn, with E. Kinney Zalesne, *Microtrends*: *The Small Forces behind Tomorrow's Big Changes* (New York: Twelve, 2007), 365.

23. "Marketing to Women," *She-conomy,* June 4, 2009, http://www.she-conomy.com/report/facts-on-women.

24. Wasik, *And Then There's This,* 13.

25. Daniela Axinte, "Is Email Dead? Facebook Thinks So," *Social Media Today,* June 20, 2010, http://www.socialmediatoday.com/smc/208714; Anderson and Wolff, "The Web Is Dead"; Sprenger, "Sun on Privacy"; Quoted in Steve Lohr, "Now Playing: Night of the Living Tech," *The New York Times,* August 22, 2010, WK1.

26. Lenski, *Human Societies: An Introduction to Macrosociology* (Boulder, CO: Paradigm Publishing, 2005).

27. Turkle, *Life on the Screen,* 268.

28. F. Scott Fitzgerald, *The Crack-Up* (New York: New Directions, 2009), 69.

CHAPTER 10

1. Shteyngart, *Super Sad True Love Story* (New York: Random House, 2010).

2. "Overview: What Is the Singularity?" The Singularity Institute, http://singinst.org/overview/whatisthesingularity.

3. Raymond Kurzweil, "The Law of Accelerating Returns," March 7, 2001, www.kurzweilai.net/the-law-of-accelerating-returns.

4. Vance, "Merely Human? That's So Yesterday," B1, B6-7.

5. Janna Anderson and Lee Rainie, "The Future of the Internet IV," Part 3, Pew Internet and American Life Project, February 19, 2010, http://www.pewinternet.org/Reports/2010/Future-of-the-Internet-IV/Part-3Gadgets.aspx.

6. Anderson and Rainie, "The Future of the Internet IV," Pew Internet and American Life Project, Part I, February 19, 2010, http://www.pewinternet.org/Reports/2010/Future-of-the-Internet-IV/Part-1Google/Intelligence.aspx.

7. Taleb, *The Black Swan* (New York: Random House, 2007), 226.

8. *The Collected Poems of W. B. Yeats,* 2nd rev. ed. (New York: Scribner, 1996).

9. Browne, *Profiles of Popular Culture* (Madison: University of Wisconsin Press, 2005), 4–5, 7.

Selected Bibliography

Anderson, Chris. *The Long Tail: Why the Future of Business Is Selling Less of More.* New York: Hyperion, 2006.

Auletta, Ken. *Googled: The End of the World as We Know It.* New York: Penguin Press, 2009.

Barlow, Aaron. *Blogging America: The New Public Sphere.* Westport, CT: Praeger, 2007.

Boehlert, Eric. *Bloggers on the Bus: How the Internet Changed Politics and the Press.* New York: Free Press, 2009.

Carr, Nicholas. *The Shallows: What the Internet Is Doing to Our Brains.* New York: W. W. Norton, 2010.

Dehanene, Stanislas. *Reading in the Brain: The Science and Evolution of a Human Invention.* New York: Viking, 2009.

Funk, Tom. *Web 2.0 and Beyond: Understanding the New Online Business Models, Trends, and Technologies.* Westport, CT: Praeger, 2009.

Geertz, Clifford. *The Interpretation of Cultures.* New York: Basic Books, 1973.

Goffman, Erving. *The Presentation of Self in Everyday Life.* Garden City, NY: Doubleday, 1959.

Haraway, Donna J. *Simians, Cyborgs, and Women: The Reinvention of Nature.* New York: Routledge, 1991.

Hebdige, Dick. *Hiding in the Light: On Images and Things.* London: Routledge, 1989.

Keen, Andrew. *The Cult of the Amateur: How Today's Internet Is Killing Our Culture.* New York: Crown, 2007.

Kuhn, Thomas S. *The Structure of Scientific Revolutions.* 3rd ed. Chicago: University of Chicago Press, 1996.

Lanier, Jaron. *You Are Not a Gadget.* New York: Alfred A. Knopf, 2010.

Lasch, Christopher. *The Culture of Narcissism.* New York: W. W. Norton, 1978.

Manjoo, Farhad. *True Enough: Learning to Live in a Post-Fact Society.* New York: Wiley, 2008.

McChesney, Robert W., and John Nichols. *The Death and Life of American Journalism: The Media Revolution That Will Begin the World Again.* Philadelphia: Nation Books, 2010.

McLuhan, Marshall. *The Gutenberg Galaxy: The Making of Typographic Man.* Toronto: University of Toronto Press, 1962.McLuhan, Marshall, and Quentin Fiore. *The Medium Is the Massage.* New York: Bantam Books, 1967.

McLuhan, Marshall, and Quentin Fiore. *Understanding Media: The Extensions of Man.* New York: Signet Books, 1964.

Negroponte, Nicholas. *Being Digital.* New York: Alfred A. Knopf, 1995.

Palfrey, John, and Urs Gasser. *Born Digital: Understanding the First Generation of Digital Natives.* New York: Basic Books, 2008.

Penn, Mark, with E. Kinney Zalesne. *Microtrends: The Small Forces Behind Tomorrow's Big Changes.* New York: Twelve, 2007.

Pogue, David. *The World According to Twitter.* New York: Black Dog & Leventhal, 2009.

Putnam, Robert D. *Bowling Alone: The Collapse and Revival of American Community.* New York: Simon & Schuster, 2000.

Rosenberg, Scott. *Say Everything: How Blogging Began, What It's Becoming, and Why It Matters.* New York: Crown, 2009.

Siegel, Lee. *Against the Machine: How the Web Is Reshaping Culture and Commerce—and Why It Matters.* New York: Spiegel & Grau, 2009.

Stone, Biz. *Who Let the Blogs Out?* New York: St. Martin's Griffin, 2004.

Taleb, Nassim Nicholas. *The Black Swan: The Impact of the Highly Improbable.* New York: Random House, 2007.

Turkle, Sherry. *Alone Together: Why We Expect More from Technology and Less from Each Other.* New York: Basic Books, 2011.

Turkle, Sherry. *Life on the Screen: Identity in the Age of the Internet.* New York: Simon & Schuster, 1995.

Wasik, Bill. *And Then There's This: How Stories Live and Die in Viral Culture.* New York: Viking, 2009.

Williams, Raymond. *Culture and Society: 1780–1950.* New York: Columbia University Press, 1983.

Williams, Raymond. *Keywords: A Vocabulary of Culture and Society.* New York: Oxford University Press, 1983.

SELECTED WEBSITES

Blogger, http://www.blogger.com
   Free publishing for blogs, instruction on creating a blog. Google-owned.
eMarketer, http://www.emarketer.com
   A business information service offering research and trend analysis on digital marketing and media.
Internet World Stats, http://www.internetstats.com
   Usage and population statistics.
Pew Research Center: Pew Internet and American Life Project, http://www.pewinternet.org
   "A nonpartisan, nonprofit 'fact tank' that provides information on the issues, attitudes and trends shaping America and the world."
Quantcast, http://www.quantcast.com
   Web analytics service.
Sysomos, http://www.sysomos.com
   Business intelligence for social media.
Technorati, http://www.technorati.com
   A blog search engine.
Twitter, http://www.twitter.com
   Free 140-character messaging zplatform.

Index

About the Author

Mary Cross is professor emerita of English at Fairleigh Dickinson University, where she was chair of the English Department. She is the author of *Madonna: A Biography* (Greenwood, 2007) and the editor of *A Century of American Icons* (Greenwood, 2002) and *Advertising and Culture: Theoretical Perspectives* (Praeger, 1996). She has taught at the University of Delaware and at Baruch College at the City University of New York.